the rhythm boys

WILLIE FRAZIER

ROY HUNTER

PHIL GRIFFIN

DWAIN DILLARD

JOHN BIDDLE

Omaha Central High's 1968 *O-Book* featured a tribute to "the rhythm boys"— but misspelled "Dwaine." Reprinted with permission of the *Omaha Central High School O-Book*.

The Rhythm Boys
of Omaha Central

*High School Basketball
at the '68 Racial Divide*

STEVE MARANTZ

With a foreword by Susie Buffett

UNIVERSITY OF NEBRASKA PRESS | LINCOLN AND LONDON

Library of Congress Cataloging-in-Publication Data

Marantz, Steve.
The rhythm boys of Omaha Central: high school
basketball at the '68 racial divide / Steve Marantz; with a
foreword by Susie Buffett.
p. cm.
Includes bibliographical references and index.
ISBN 978-0-8032-3434-5 (pbk.: alk. paper)
1. Omaha Central High School (Omaha, Neb.)—Basketball—History. 2. Omaha Central Eagles (Basketball
team)—History. 3. African American basketball players—Nebraska—Omaha—History. 4. Discrimination
in sports—Nebraska—Omaha—History. 5. Racism
in sports—Nebraska—Omaha—History. 6. Basketball—Nebraska—Omaha—History. I. Title.
GV885.73.O63M37 2011
796.323'6309782254—dc22
2010025880

Set in Minion by Kim Essman.

Designed by Ray W. Boeche.

To Dennis Marantz, class of '66, and all brothers and sisters

This is no fiction; this is no act
This is real, it's a fact
Smokey Robinson and the Miracles

Contents

Foreword

Susie Buffett

I graduated from Omaha Central High School in 1971, the year Dr. Gaylord Moller called the worst of his career as principal. The reason? Racial tension—ignited in 1968 by events chronicled in *The Rhythm Boys of Omaha Central*—was off the chart.

When Doc told me that, years later, I was surprised. From my perspective, race relations had not been that bad. The racial tension of the late sixties and early seventies was something I didn't feel inside the school—in spite of the fact that our cafeterias were segregated, by choice, not rule. Whites and blacks mixed in homeroom, choir, and various other activities, so it didn't feel to me like a segregated or tense environment.

The diversity at Central was, to me, really wonderful. It provided a "real life" education that was in some ways better and more important than the academic education.

I was not unaware of segregation, hate, and prejudice in the larger world. I grew up in a house with parents (particularly my mother, Susan Thompson Buffett, president of the Central High School class of 1950, who spent time in north Omaha working with community groups such as Head Start, Boys Club, and the Wesley House. I remember being stopped by the police on several occasions for "driving while white" in north Omaha. It made my mother furious.

My best friend in high school was Debbie Jacobson, whose older sister, Diane, is mentioned in *The Rhythm Boys of Omaha Central*. Diane and Delmar Givehand were the interracial couple I was most aware of—and I remember many conversations with Debbie discussing her parents' unhappiness about Diane and Delmar's relationship.

And on several occasions, I remember sneaking a Jewish friend, Ann Reinglas, out of her basement window to go out with a decidedly un-Jewish Jim Crosby. Another huge secret—Julie Bernstein was dating John Carey, a straight-up goy. Julie asked me to go to prom with John because her mother would not allow them to see each other. I did this mitzvah for her and then spent the night at her house to give her every detail of the evening.

At the same time we were pulling Ann out of her basement window, my father was working to get a Jewish friend, Nick Newman, admitted to the gentile-only Omaha Club—a story recounted in this book. Dinner-table conversation in our house was frequently about civil rights—whether it be racial or religious. And my parents were not people who just talked about these issues—they were in the neighborhoods and they worked tirelessly for social justice. They influenced me to teach sewing in the housing projects at Thirty-third and Parker, and to volunteer at Head Start during the summers of my high school years.

As much as I felt at the time that things were not as bad as Dr. Moller said, I also know that my perspective was one of a white girl living in a safe neighborhood, unaffected by the riots and fires that were a reality for my black classmates.

One of my classmates was Brenda Warren Council. She is an African American woman who, in addition to being a lawyer, has served as president of the Omaha School Board, was a member of the city council, and currently serves as a senator in the Nebraska State Legislature. She also ran twice for mayor of Omaha—a black female Democrat, no less—and lost her second bid by only 735 votes.

We remain close friends and have talked about how her perspective in high school differed from mine. We have also talked about how some things have changed—but many things haven't. To this day, our reunions are segregated, not because the committee doesn't invite everyone but because most of the black kids from my class attend their own reunion. If you ask them why, they will tell you that they attend a reunion of Horace Mann Junior High, an all-black school on the Near North Side. The Horace Mann reunion includes their friends who later attended Tech High and North High, as well as Central.

This is true. But it does not explain why they do not attend their Central reunion, and it makes me wonder if things weren't more deeply segregated than I realized when I was in high school. As an adult I can see now that the tension clearly affected the black kids more than the white kids, and they felt more bonded to each other than to the concept of diversity. It makes me sad that things didn't change in a way that would have made an integrated reunion a reality—that everyone would have wanted to be together—but I understand why it is the way it is.

Some things described in *The Rhythm Boys* have changed. Bagel, as one Omaha neighborhood was known, doesn't exist. The hallways at Central look different. The demographics have changed—white flight and busing caused people to move west. The school has a much higher black population today and a much smaller Jewish population. There are interracial couples and no one looks twice—or cares. Students opt in to Central from every part of the city, seeking diversity, an excellent college prep education, or both. And Central is still the largest high school in the state.

I believe strongly that Central is the best high school in the country—a broad statement but I believe it. It's a rare place—a school in the middle of downtown with a mixed group of kids, racially and socioeconomically—and still excellent academically. There are few, if any, urban public high schools left in the country that can claim to provide an excellent education for their students. And, as I said earlier, the "real life" education matters as much as the academic piece.

It's not perfect. In a two-county area where 77 percent of African American children live in poverty, a school like Central has challenges. Many of us work every day to address those challenges and make Central—and the world, really—a better place. I am proud that my two children were the fifth generation in my family—after me, my mother, and my dad's father and grandfather—to attend Central.

The school's basketball tradition, described in Steve Marantz's account of *The Rhythm Boys of Omaha Central*, remains strong. I still go to the basketball games (we took state three years in a row recently and are seeded number ONE as I write this!). The gym on game night is one of the most diverse places in the city of Omaha and that makes it feel like one of the most hopeful places. I have to stop and think if the starting lineup for Central is all black. Or is it mixed? I don't know. And I don't care. And, really, neither does anyone else in the gym.

Prologue

In March 1968, two high school basketball teams played for the Nebraska state championship, a contest with decades of wholesome tradition. But this game was different.

A few days earlier former Alabama governor George C. Wallace had come to Omaha to campaign for president. He brought the Deep South — "segregation now, segregation tomorrow, segregation forever" and the jackboots of Selma — and set it down two blocks from Omaha Central High School. His searing rhetoric scalded the sensibilities of many, including eighteen-year-old Dwaine Dillard, Central's African American basketball superstar.

Eye-to-eye at tipoff were forces that propelled Wallace and tore at the sixties: white and black, tradition and change, structure and improvisation. Race and politics — served up on a hardwood floor.

When Central and Lincoln Northeast met in the final, the back story was pure Hollywood.

Dillard threw an elbow for black power and collided with the presidential campaign. Bigwigs, cops, and politicians gnashed their hands and wrung their teeth. Teenagers rebelled, came of age, and lost their innocence — all at once. Before it was over blood was spilled, tears were shed, arrests were made, and hoops were played.

I was there and I'll never forget it.

But then, it's not hard to remember the Rhythm Boys, as Dillard and his teammates were known. Their spirit lives at the unmarked crossroads of youth, adulthood, justice, and morality.

Their nickname captured who they were and what they did on a basketball court. Sons of Omaha's inner city, at the climax of the civil rights movement, their game personified their generation: exuberant, hopeful, and rebellious. So, too, their star-crossed fate.

The story of the Rhythm Boys, a team of its time, is for all seasons.

It is also the story of Omaha Central High in 1968, ten years after African American students integrated another Central High, in Little Rock, Arkansas, under the protection of federal troops. There were, and are, hundreds of Central Highs across America, built when cities were young, emblems of a noble idea, public education, vulnerable to demagogues. This one belongs to all, as that epic year belongs to the ages.

First Bell

In 1967, Omaha Central High opened for the first day of class on Tuesday, September 5, the day after Labor Day, at the end of the Summer of Love.

Teenagers from the Midwest river city arose, brushed their teeth, gulped cereal, and got off to school.

From the Near North Side, the African American neighborhood, came Dwaine Dillard, an eighteen-year-old senior, and Central's resident celebrity.

In an era dominated by iconic centers—Bill Russell and Wilt Chamberlain in the NBA, Lew Alcindor at dynastic UCLA—Dillard was exactly that—a dominant center and icon—at Central High.

He was six foot seven, two hundred pounds, black and beautiful, with a smooth burnished complexion, large dark eyes, and a long slender torso he propelled with grace and assurance. In the last days before the voluminous Afro, his hair was medium length, trim and neat.

When Dillard walked through the west entrance, accompanied by his teammates, Willie Frazier and John Biddle, eyes turned, and the sea of bodies parted. Palms were extended, skin was exchanged, and Dillard radiated warmth and noblesse oblige.

Among the crowd around the "sacred C," a polished inlay on the floor of the west foyer, were Jeff Krum and Harvey Josin, two Jewish teammates of Dillard's; Vikki Dollis, a pretty cheerleader and student-council member with blonde hair and sad eyes; and Sue Glyn, a slender brunette who was Frazier's girlfriend. Across the courtyard, in the east foyer, near the life-size Liberty Bell replica, two more of Dillard's teammates, Roy Hunter and Phil Griffin, exchanged greetings.

A warning bell rang at 8:16 a.m., and at first bell, 8:20 a.m., students were in their homerooms for an initial eleven-minute period. In room 347, Warren Marquiss, age forty-six, a biology teacher by day, and varsity basketball coach by afternoon and evening, counted attendance.

In a first-floor office overlooking Twentieth Street, J. Arthur Nelson, white-haired, round, and bespectacled, settled at his desk with a grunt. At sixty-seven, Nelson was in his twenty-fourth year as principal, lord of all except gravity.

Perched on a hill, above downtown Omaha, Central High was a vision from antiquity, with arches, columns, cornices, pilasters, and pediments — all symmetrical and ordered.

To a student, that's how it felt, too. I was there, a sixteen-year-old junior, an acolyte at the temple.

Central was Omaha's first and oldest high school, founded in 1859, in the straggly village on the edge of the prairie, eight years before Nebraska became a state. The gray cornerstone of the Renaissance Revival architecture was laid in 1900, the year John Arthur Nelson was born on a Nebraska farm. Nelson grew up to personify the architecture, and much that the sixties disdained.

Central High—a vision from antiquity, symmetrical and ordered. Reprinted with permission of the *Omaha World-Herald*.

A former debate coach—rational, stern, and demanding—he was a mythical figure, whose word was final at a time when principals commanded the power of Zeus. Nelson's signature aphorism, "A word to the wise is sufficient," was intoned less as advice than a warning. "He was so intimidating that even veteran faculty were scared to death of him," recalled Dr. Gaylord Moller, then assistant principal.

The same went for students. In the fall of 1967, 2,377 students were enrolled, taught by ninety-four teachers. Nearly one-fifth of the students were black, about one-fourth were Jewish, and the rest were ethnic and vanilla whites, Catholics, and Protestants. Omaha was a city of neighborhoods and many were represented: Near North Side, Little Italy, Field Club, Hanscom Park, Robin Hill, Dundee, Happy Hollow, Elmwood, Fairacres, and Bagel. Central was described as a melting pot, though the social temperature was uneven at best.

It was less a melting pot than a buffet, the kind of school where a black kid from the projects, the nephew of a convicted murderer, could be seated next to the son of a Jewish merchant, who had employed the murder victim.

Which is what happened to Delmar Givehand when he enrolled as a freshman.

"I got to talking with this kid and mentioned that my uncle, Luther Wilson, was in prison," Givehand recalled. "He said, 'Yeah, my dad owns the market where he shot so-and-so.'"

It was also the kind of school where a white student from an ethnic neighborhood met blacks for the first time, as was the case with John Gaines, who grew up in south Omaha, in Sheeleytown, named after two Irish brothers who founded one of the city's first packinghouses.

"At my barbershop a polack sitting over here made a crack about a dago sitting over there, and a Czech called somebody a bohunk, and a German told an Irish joke," Gaines recalled. "There was a lot of diversity, except there were no blacks."

Race and class blended into the usual milieu of cliques and personalities: jocks, cheerleaders, brains, nerds, preppies, slobs, sluts, and greasers. All were subject to the authority imposed by Nelson. The school had its routine and traditions. Change occurred at the margins, in small measure, but in the rites and rituals of Central, September 1967 could have been 1957 or 1947.

The *Purple and White Handbook*, a list of rules and regulations, included a grooming code: "'Ducktails,' 'Beatle,' and other 'elaborate' hair styles are prohibited. Boys will be clean-shaven. Shirts and coat collars will be turned down. All shirt buttons will be buttoned, except for the collar button and cuff buttons if the sleeves are rolled up."

Belts were required—boys who did not wear a belt were given the option of "renting one" or sitting in the office on an unexcused absence. Girls were prohibited from wearing slacks: "Obviously unusual or unorthodox dress will not be tolerated."

The handbook defined Central's mission, in prose Nelson might have borrowed from Charles Darwin:

Just as it's always been and more than likely always will be, this is a harsh world for most of us when we're out on our own. It is a world of fierce competition with those of us who are prepared and are getting ahead. Today you are planning for tomorrow. Will your life be rich and purposeful, or will you drift with the winds of time? You are beginning now to make that choice.

School began in time-honored fashion, as new freshmen and sophomores stumbled through the labyrinth and got the hang of the place. The west entrance faced the Joslyn Art Museum; the east entrance faced downtown and, in the distance, the Missouri River; and the south entrance faced Dodge Street, Omaha's main thoroughfare.

The ground, second, and third floors surrounded an interior courtyard with a rectangle of hallways. Classrooms and study halls faced outward, toward the streets, while faculty offices faced the courtyard. On the north side was a small but elegant theater/auditorium with wooden seats, and a bandbox of a gym. Inside the east entrance, in the foyer, was a Liberty Bell replica. Beneath the gym were locker rooms with steam pipes that hissed and shower rooms crusted with mold.

Principal J. Arthur Nelson: "A word to the wise is sufficient." Reprinted with permission of the *Omaha Central High School O-Book*.

The wooden hallways creaked. Wooden lockers, carved upon by generations past, sometimes shut, and sometimes didn't. There were separate stairs for boys and girls, because the restrooms on the stair landings did not have doors. It was easy to intentionally forget and go up or down the stairway of the opposite sex.

The interior courtyard was a convenient shortcut whose doors opened in good weather, though its pigeon droppings required an agile step.

Two cafeterias were on the fourth floor, on the north and west sides. Whites tended to use one, and blacks used the other, a de facto division that tripped up new students once or twice before they figured it out. If a student climbed four flights from a basement classroom to a cafeteria, he or she might be too winded to care.

Just inside the west entrance, where students gathered before the first bell, the "sacred C" was not supposed to be walked upon. An editorial in the student newspaper, the *Register*, in October, urged students to observe the tradition, which started in 1959 when the C was laid.

"It's a deep shame to see all the students who are careless or in a hurry to step on the 'C' without any regards as to what they are doing," the *Register* scolded, in a fair imitation of Nelson.

The *Register* profiled its editor, Paul Lubetkin, in November.

"Newspapers will eventually be outdated," Lubetkin said. "They will become anachronisms and will have a very limited place in society that demands greater speed, depth, and diversity."

At Central it was okay to be as geeky as the *Register*, and as smart as Lubetkin. His class would produce ten National Merit semifinalists and two scholarship winners, while the math team, taught by the estimable Virginia Lee Pratt, and chess team would win their fourth straight state championships.

Such were the expectations of Nelson, who liked to call Central "the Boston Latin School of Nebraska," a reference to the nation's oldest public school, which held that classics were the basis of an educated mind. Under Nelson, in the 1950s, Central had pioneered Advanced Placement courses that awarded college credits to ambitious seniors. His reputation was such that his personal phone call to an Ivy League university virtually guaranteed admission for a Central senior. In the 1960s, Central ranked among top American high schools, as measured by

National Merit test results and an annual University of Chicago academic survey. Small wonder, as students were urged to do two hours of homework for each one-hour course.

"The atmosphere was incredible," recalled Bob Cain, who taught English at Central from 1961 to 1972. "You walked in and all eyes were on the teacher. And they listened to what you said."

English required six teacher-assigned themes per semester, and if a student came up one short, he or she failed. Juniors were taught exposition, while seniors learned argumentation and read John Milton's epic poem, *Paradise Lost*, about Lucifer's fall from grace. Everybody adhered to the *Style Book* canon written in 1921 and revised in 1935 by Sara Vore Taylor, the English Department head whose instructions were so punctilious as to stipulate which side of theme paper should be perforated—left.

As school geared up so did extracurricular activity. Those of musical bent joined pit orchestra, dance band, concert band, chamber choir, junior choir, mixed chorus, girls' glee, and A Cappella Choir. The prestigious A Cappella, whose ninety-seven members wore distinctive blue blazers, started rehearsals for its December musical, *110 in the Shade*.

Also in rehearsal was *The Chalk Garden*, the fall play of the Central High Players. Another club, Thespians, made ready for a spring play, *The Devil and Daniel Webster*. All musicians and performers set their sights on the annual Road Show, a twenty-two-act variety show scheduled for three days in March.

Clubs organized around domestic relations and political science, human relations, stamp and coin, chess, audiovisual, future nurses and future physicians, Greenwich Village, debate, math, literature, library, homemaking, outdoorsmen, German,

French, Inter-American, and Junior Classical League. The latter explored art and literature of ancient Greece and Rome and was Central's oldest club, founded in 1903. Not surprisingly, it was one of Nelson's favorites.

As the Vietnam War escalated that fall, those of military bent—still trusting and dutiful—joined Reserve Officer Training Corps, Color Guard, Queen's Lancers, King's Hussars, Crack Squad, Cadet Police, rifle team, rifle club, and Commissioned Officers Club, with an eye toward the Military Ball in February.

Nelson was ambivalent about sports, his instinctive disdain offset by their usefulness in public relations and marketing. Hampered by inadequate facilities, varsity, junior varsity, and reserve football teams started their seasons, and cross-country got underway.

Cheerleading began for girls, as Vikki Dollis, who had kept a diary since fifth grade, noted in her entry for September 8:

Today was a pretty exciting day, beginning with the pep rally we cheered for before school. It wasn't really that scary and I can only remember the heat now. That was the main problem all day—wearing wool outfits when it was 85 degrees out. The game I anticipated to be so wonderful turned out quite disappointing. Besides being boring because we lost 38–0, I was sweating to death and I had horrible pains all over and mainly in the feet. I came right home after the game and took a hot bath to go to bed. I feel good now—awful tomorrow.

Athletic options for girls were limited. Central had a group called the Girls Athletic Association, which offered shuffleboard, table tennis, volleyball, bowling, and basketball.

Jo Wagner, a cheerleader, and Bob Taylor, a football player, were chosen homecoming queen and king at a dance at the Holiday Inn, with music by the Wonders.

Mundane events unfolded: the courtyard was cleaned of pigeon droppings, new trophy cases were built on the first floor, and the honor-roll system was overhauled.

On the surface Central moved through the fall semester as it had since Nelson became principal in 1944, ordered, disciplined, and impregnable. But a closer look revealed an undercurrent of . . . change!

The *Register*, in a November editorial, again urged students to honor tradition. The *Register* cited a *Wall Street Journal* editorial that had called the hippie movement a "triumph of vulgarity." The *Journal* had written that while there were few actual hippies, many teenagers shared their careless attitude. To which the *Register* added, "These attitudes in Central life constitute not caring about the school—what it represents or how they represent it. Traditions are disregarded by many, little respect is given to teachers or administration."

The weary voice of an ailing and aging principal echoed through the piece. Few students, or even faculty, knew of Nelson's physical decline. He had been ill, with failing eyesight. The co-assistant principals, Gaylord Moller and Clifford Dale, had taken control in matters of discipline. Their reports did not comfort him—increased tardiness, disregard of rules, abuse of property, and brazen disrespect of authority. A new student subset—social and political activists—was vocal. Black students had specific complaints about the curriculum and faculty; one black girl was suspended for wearing a sweatshirt that read "Sock It To Me—Black Power." Something was happening that wasn't exactly clear.

"I don't know what to do," Nelson told Moller.

Nelson's confusion was generational and cultural. He had built a moat around Central to keep out the sixties. But the onslaught of popular culture, as depicted by four of the five films nominated for Best Picture in January 1968, was irresistible and irreversible. *The Graduate* was about a college graduate alienated from his white, affluent, and "plastics" world. *Bonnie and Clyde* celebrated the notion of the antihero. *Guess Who's Coming to Dinner?* broached the taboo of biracial love. *In the Heat of the Night* offered the spectacle of a black detective slapping a white Southern aristocrat.

The scene must have jarred Nelson, if indeed he saw it. Among his confidantes, he referred to blacks as "Smoky Swedes."

"That was his slang term—he would say it to one of us with a chuckle," recalled Dan Daly, who taught English at Central from 1962 until his retirement in 1999, and was hired by Nelson. "He was a racist. But most people of his age, at that time, were. It's not that they were evil—they grew up that way."

Nelson long had made peace with institutional racism. Frank Tirro, Central High class of '53, wanted to attend Yale, only to be told by Nelson that he was not a "Yale type" because he was of Italian descent. Tirro went to Cornell, then the University of Nebraska, and earned a doctorate from the University of Chicago. In 1980 he became a professor at the Yale School of Music.

Jane Fellman, class of '56, wanted to attend Northwestern, but Nelson discouraged her because it had a quota on Jewish admissions. He urged her to apply to Michigan, and she refused. He gave in, recommended her for Northwestern, and she was accepted.

"I don't think he was racist, but his actions were," recalled Richard Fellman, Jane's brother.

Nelson was a member of an Omaha church infamous for racism among some members. Augustana Lutheran, where Nelson had belonged since 1938 and had served as superintendent of the Sunday school, not two miles from Central, was the subject of a film documentary, *A Time for Burning*. Lutheran Film Associates, an outgrowth of the mainstream Lutheran Church, commissioned the film in 1965 and had anticipated a rosy affirmation of Christian values.

Instead, the film shocked viewers in its portrayal of genteel racism among Augustana's all-white parishioners. A new and earnest young pastor from Minnesota, L. William Youngdahl, had wanted to institute contact—religious and cultural—with fellow black Lutherans. But the members were skeptical, and Youngdahl found himself on the defensive. When Youngdahl persisted in his efforts, the church governing council forced him to resign. The council informed Youngdahl that he was "a mismatch" with Augustana and that members were alienated because he did not preach the Gospel as they conceived it.

A Time for Burning was deemed too controversial by the three broadcast networks before it was aired on public television in 1966. Filmmaker William C. Jersey's work of cinema verité was nominated as Best Documentary Feature for the 1967 Academy Awards.

Nelson's position on Youngdahl's initiative was not reported in the documentary, nor does he appear in any of the scenes. But if his management of Central High was an indication, he most certainly opposed it. In 1967 the Central faculty included just one black teacher, Wilda Stephenson, who taught business and typing.

The complexion of the faculty under Nelson had been conspicuous for years. Tom Brokaw, in his history of the 1960s, *Boom!*, wrote about the start of his broadcast news career in Omaha in 1962. His wife, Meredith, taught English at Central.

Brokaw described Central as "the city's most acclaimed high school," and added, "it was a magnet for the city's best and brightest kids because of its strong college prep curriculum, but it also served the black neighborhoods of the Near North Side."

Yet, Brokaw wrote, his wife "cannot remember a black faculty member."

The racial makeup of the faculty was not the only reason for black students to be circumspect. The English curriculum included the play *Emperor Jones*, in which a racial slur is used repeatedly. There was no African American history course, and virtually no African American narrative in traditional history courses.

The relative affluence of white students was a daily reminder of de facto caste. Each morning the parking lot filled up with cars driven by white teenagers. Few black students drove to school, and few black parents could afford the luxury cars in which white parents dropped off their children. Many black students hiked the two or three miles from the Near North Side.

But it was Nelson's "all-white faculty minus one" that sent the strongest message to black students. And not only the faculty—the two assistant principals, guidance director, two senior counselors, and the nurse were white, as were the twenty-three women who comprised the office and cafeteria staffs.

"School was more comfortable for the white kids," recalled John Biddle. "It more resembled home for them—they had relationships with teachers and administrators—older people who looked over them."

Black students attended Central in spite of the institutional racism practiced by Nelson. Some were legacies, such as Biddle, who followed two older sisters. Another legacy, Biddle's teammate Roy Hunter, lived a few blocks from North High, on Ames Avenue, but trekked a far greater distance to Central, as had his older brother, Jim Hunter.

Others came because it was a proven gateway to college—and a toehold on the American Dream. Steve Moss, a black member of the basketball team, grew up in the inner city with his eyes on Creighton University, the Jesuit school whose campus virtually abutted Central. Moss started out at Tech High, until he figured that his best route to Creighton was through Central.

"Central was a beacon school," Moss recalled. "If you wanted to go to college that's what stood out."

Institutional racism, Moss recalled, was "a subtle thing everybody had to deal with."

In the fall of 1965, Delmar Givehand, as a freshman, wandered into the "white" cafeteria, and realized he was the only black student around. Raised in a Near North Side project, Givehand was curious about whites. He returned to the "white" cafeteria the next day and the next, until one day he went to sit down and found a sign: "This cafeteria is segregated." The sign galvanized black students.

"Shortly after that a number of black students started eating in that cafeteria," Givehand recalled.

That same year several Jewish students—Bob Guss, Bob Jacobson, Barry Kaiman, Jerry Raznick, Gary Soiref, and Ira Fox, all in the class of '68—were rowdy at lunch. George Andrews, a football coach who served as cafeteria monitor, meted out a peculiar punishment. He ordered them to the "black" cafeteria—for the rest of the school year.

Throughout most of Nelson's tenure, black students had accounted for 10 percent or less of the student body. But in the mid-1960s that figure rose to between 15 and 20 percent, as more black students broadened their horizons and sought Central's college-prep curriculum.

This shift troubled Nelson, as evidenced by his couched—yet obvious—complaints to district administrators. As far back as 1957, in his annual report to the superintendent, Nelson had cited as a problem absence and tardiness "from one area of town," which "amounts to a philosophy of life." His 1961 report cited "the problem of having youngsters in the senior class who really can do very little better than eighth-grade work along the side of people who have mastered calculus and analytics."

His 1962 report began, "Perhaps this report should not be written, for I am afraid that it represents my personal bitterness over frustrations over problems that have not been met." One problem he cited was the "vast numbers of students [who] come to us who are not by native intelligence endowed with the ability to do college work."

His 1963 report cited "the problem of non-academic even non-reading students, in a school that is largely college preparatory, with little opportunity to expand its vocational program." In his 1964 report, Nelson wrote of "two groups in school not capable of carrying the academic load of the school." His 1965 report again stated, "We are getting a larger number who by aptitude are not capable of doing college preparatory work or the work of vocation as we do have."

Nelson pressed the superintendent's office for expanded vocational resources. In 1965 he made the first of several requests for updated athletic facilities. Such requests masked his disappointment and frustration over a moribund plan to construct a new Central High, to the west, near the University of Nebraska at Omaha, which had been discussed since the mid-1950s. That had been his dream, hinted at in his 1963 report, when he urged that "the possibility and feasibility of moving Central be explored."

His 1966 report offered a glimpse of his waning energy, as well as front-office intrigue, as he wrote, "I am sure that the anticipation of 'the king is dead, long live the king' is causing some problems."

By 1967, Nelson seemed alienated from even the new hires on his own faculty. His report cited as a problem the inability to recruit "faculty who are professional, even missionary in spirit, and who have sufficient scholarship to speak, write, and spell with high proficiency, and who recognize that standards do matter."

Nelson's moat to keep out the sixties—his dated set of standards—was not wide or deep enough. It could not keep out the backlash against the war in Vietnam, or the riots that had erupted in dozens of inner cities, Omaha's included. It could not deter the hippie counterculture that mocked the world Nelson tried to preserve at Central.

The very air Nelson breathed—curled with a faint whiff of pot—had changed.

"There were times when—I hate to say it—he just couldn't handle it," Moller recalled.

In the December 20, 1967, issue of the *Register* an article ran under the headline "A Christmas Message":

Do unto others as you would have them do unto you. As I write this last Christmas message, the years seem to have made it so apparent that the grave problems of our times could be solved if all people heeded this simple biblical sermon . . . an essential point of the truly great religions of the world. May it be granted to you to have this wisdom and understanding.

Thus, J. Arthur Nelson announced his retirement.

In the same issue appeared another headline: "Cagers to Open New Campaign." The basketball team was about to open its season, led by Dillard, far and away the best player in the state. Dillard intended to ignore Nelson's advice because that was what teenagers did with adult advice. He would do unto others an excellence of hoops that could not easily be returned. But Dillard also would inflict upon himself what an opponent could not—infamy.

Nelson and Dillard shared a moment in history, headed in opposite directions. As Nelson fled the cultural *zeitgeist*, Dillard rushed to meet it. Nelson's role in Central mythology was almost complete. Dillard's was about to begin.

2

Tears of a Clown

Dwaine Rufus Dillard was a mystery. And is.

At Central everybody knew who Dillard was. But nobody knew him—not even himself.

His most public side cavorted on the grand stage of high school athletic stardom. As Dillard's senior year began he was the best high school basketball player in Nebraska, and for all anybody knew, America. One national publication named him to its preseason All-American third team, thus "placing him as one of the top 15 cagers in the nation," reported the *Central High Register.*

"Some think he is the best prep cager Nebraska has ever seen," wrote student reporter David J. Katz.

But if his legacy had been about basketball only, he would have been no different than other stars of other eras. The only aspect of his game that foreshadowed his fate was his mercurial temperament. "He was our best player but he was our biggest screw-up, too," recalled Phil Griffin, a teammate.

In the hallways of Omaha's oldest and most acclaimed high school he presented an affable and mischievous front, even as he puzzled in its classrooms and addressed teachers as "Sir" and "Ma'am."

A nocturnal side, less visible, was drawn to bars and gambling dens.

A private side, known to intimates, alternated from sweet to cruel.

And then there was something deep within—scarred and painful and dangerous. Most every eighteen-year-old has had it, and will. The passage from adolescence to adulthood sails across this strait of self-reckoning. In the first week of March 1968, Dillard made his passage, and detoured to history.

He was named after his father—sort of.

When he was born on March 9, 1949, Rufus Dwaine Dillard anointed him.

"Rufus Dwaine Dillard Jr.," his father announced.

His mother objected.

"One Rufus is enough."

They settled on Dwaine Rufus. He was the first child of Phyllis Smith, who was not quite sixteen, a junior at Omaha South High. "Dwaine was my sixteenth birthday present," she recalled. His size came from her side, though at birth he was an ordinary six pounds and twenty-one inches. Her father, Sam Smith, a Mississippi transplant, was tall and large, her brother and two sisters were tall, and Phyllis stood at five foot six.

Dwaine Rufus became his father's delight, and as a little boy reveled in his father's warmth and affection. Rufus Dillard's family had come from rural Arkansas before World War II to work in the booming stockyards on Omaha's South Side. Rufus worked in a packinghouse for a short time before he enlisted in the U.S. Army. He took his young family on an odyssey through military bases in the Midwest and South

Dwaine Rufus Dillard, son of Rufus Dwaine Dillard. Photo courtesy of Carlos Dillard.

as Phyllis gave birth to four more children. When Rufus was sent to Germany, Phyllis declined to follow and rented a small house close to the Southside Terrace projects, a black enclave near the stockyards. Her father, a packinghouse worker, and mother, a hospital cook, helped her manage.

Phyllis was an accomplished cook and musician. She fed her brood well, and was known to neighbors and friends for her generous kitchen. She played the organ at Union Memorial United Methodist Church and required her children, Dwaine included, to sing in the choir at Bethel Baptist Church. Dillard attended the Indian Hills and Marrs elementary schools and was an average student, at least in the early grades. He preferred the Woodson Center, a neighborhood settlement house where he picked up a basketball for the first time, and came to trust Alice Wilson, the much-beloved director.

One spring Phyllis took ill and was sent to a military hospital in Colorado for treatment. With Rufus in Germany, the children were placed in foster homes for several months.

"I lived with a foster family on Twenty-sixth and Binney," Dillard recalled. "I didn't like it. I slept under the bed, on the hard floor, because of the stress. After awhile my grandmother came and got me and my brother."

Phyllis recovered and resumed care of her children. Soon Phyllis concluded that Rufus, who frequented brothels, "was not the daddy of the year." The marriage broke apart when Dwaine Rufus was ten.

"He divorced my mother and moved out of Omaha," Dillard recalled. "For a long time I thought he would come back."

Rufus Dwaine's departure left a chilly void in his oldest son's upbringing. After he was gone, Phyllis crisscrossed the city on buses to clean and cook for white families in affluent neighborhoods, accepted help from her parents, and received welfare.

Absent his father, Dwaine Rufus began to act out.

"I was a pretty rough kid—I got into trouble constantly," Dillard recalled. "I wasn't a bad kid—it was just the influence I had in the projects. Kids got into a lot of mischief, like throwing eggs and playing hooky from school. When you played hooky the railroad detectives came to get you—it was a cat-and-mouse game."

By fifth or sixth grade, Dillard recalled, he was persona non grata at school.

"All the bad kids like me were put in the basement," he recalled. "We weren't allowed to socialize with the others."

Accounts of Dillard's early adolescence are vague. At twelve he and his younger brother, Carlos, went to live with Rufus Dwaine in Kansas City, but stayed only a short time. Dwaine Rufus added five inches, overnight it seemed, and became lean and lanky, built for basketball. His shoe size was twelve, and a year later, thirteen. At some point his classroom performance, hampered by a reading disability and what was not yet labeled as "attention deficit disorder," caused him to repeat a grade.

At home, Phyllis coddled her younger children, yet was strict and distant with Dwaine. If he stayed out too late she locked the door, and he crawled in through a window left open by his younger siblings.

He tried to father the younger children. Carlos remembered that Dwaine was protective though not outwardly affectionate. As a child, afraid of the dark, Carlos asked Dwaine to share his bed—with Carlos on the wall side.

"He was humongous to me," Carlos said. "He seemed like he wasn't scared of anything. He would go into the darkest places without turning on the lights."

As Carlos got older he knew Dwaine had his back.

"He acted like he wasn't watching but he never let me get too far from his watchful eye," Carlos said.

Meanwhile, his father had remarried in California and worked as a cook at a state prison. Dwaine Rufus longed to rejoin Rufus Dwaine, which is how he came to attend Ravenswood High School in East Palo Alto, California.

"I started varsity in the ninth grade there and did real well," Dillard recalled.

But Dillard's second reunion with his father was short-lived. Something drove them apart—possibly Dillard's tense relationship with his stepmother. "One day I looked up and he was back," his mother recalled. "I have no idea what happened and he didn't say."

Dillard returned dispirited and determined to forget his father. In the summer of 1965, Warren Marquiss, Central's longtime basketball coach, spotted him on a court, all six feet five inches, and liked what he saw. Dillard was drawn to the slight, professorial coach, father of four, then in his mid-forties. The two clicked, and Dillard enrolled at Central as a sixteen-year-old sophomore.

"I was having a little problem, and he took me under his wing," Dillard recalled.

He began to spend more time at the home of his paternal grandmother, Zillia Hood, on the Near North Side, Omaha's inner city. Her house at Twenty-fourth and Sprague was more convenient to Central and less crowded than Phyllis's apartment, where four more children were underfoot, and she had become Phyllis Briggs. Dillard liked that his grandmother, who had logged thirty-four years at the Swift and Company packinghouse, did not monitor his schedule. He did not like that Hood drank, or that her husband, an alcoholic, was abusive to her.

Due to transfer rules, Dillard wasn't eligible to play until the second semester. His impact was immediate. An ordinary squad before his arrival, Central won six straight games and advanced to the quarterfinal of the state tournament. It lost by one point to the eventual and repeat champion, Boys Town, on a last-second shot, but Dillard's legend was launched. In seven games Dillard averaged 11.4 points, with a 19-point, 11-rebound effort against South High.

"With the return of (Ben) Brown, Dillard, and Mark Wilson the Eagles should be next year's state champions," crowed the 1966 *O-Book*, Central's yearbook.

In the summer of 1966 Dillard honed his skills and built strength and endurance. On playground asphalt, Dillard went up against Omaha's best—NBA star Bob Boozer, future ABA star Ron Boone, and former Tech High star Fred Hare. "He took on the iron," recalled John Biddle. "It made him tougher and better."

It should have been a summer to savor imminent stardom. Instead, it was long and hot.

On July 3, 1966, with the temperature at 103 degrees, the Near North Side erupted in violence, frustration, and civil disorder. Omaha's inner city was not the first to riot in the 1960s, or the last. But it was typical, in that its residents were fed up with hostile police and city officials, crumbling schools, housing, and services, lack of jobs and economic opportunity, and pervasive social and cultural degradation.

Nebraska's governor, Frank B. Morrison, blamed the outbreak on "an environment unfit for human habitation." He said the problems had been neglected for many years and had become "acute."

The disturbance lasted three days. At one point, four thousand people gathered near the riot epicenter of Twenty-fourth and Lake. On the third night, steel-helmeted Nebraska National Guardsmen were called in to assist police. Windows were broken, stores were looted and burned, and gangs of youth marauded through the streets. Among those youth was Dillard.

"We broke into a TV repair shop," Dillard recalled. "Then we went down to a department store, at Sixteenth and Cuming, and broke into that."

Dillard was arrested, along with about 120 others, most of them teenagers. Eventually the burglary charge was dropped, but the incident branded Dillard, even as it anticipated a greater drama to come. He was more than the sum of his baskets, blocked shots, and rebounds. There was anger in him.

School resumed and Dillard, with his attention back on basketball, blossomed into a star. By February 1967 Dillard was, wrote *Register* sports editor Mike Cain, "perhaps the best in the state and the best Central has ever seen."

As an athlete Dillard was fast, strong, and dexterous. At practices he would lift himself into a handstand, to the amazement of his teammates and coaches.

"Then he walked around the gym on his hands," recalled Jim Martin, the junior varsity coach. "For a guy that tall to have that balance and strength and coordination—it was fabulous."

As a competitor he was ferocious. A younger and smaller friend, Calvin Brown (Tech High class of '70), recalled that once he wrestled with Dillard at a neighborhood park. Brown got underneath Dillard, lifted, and pinned him. Dillard sprang up, furious. Later, at a nearby basketball court, Dillard contested Brown's shots with a vengeance.

"He thought he could swat my shot and knock me on my head," Brown recalled. "I needed a good step on him to stay in one piece."

A younger Central player, Lindbergh White, remembered a practice in which he ran a fast break at Dillard. As White drove the right side, Dillard eyed him from the middle of the key. The look on Dillard's face, White recalled, was predatory.

Dwaine Dillard (*bottom*) and Willie Frazier started as juniors. Reprinted with permission of the *Omaha Central High School O-Book*.

"He was going to block my shot or take me out of the play," White recalled.

A behind-the-back pass foiled Dillard, but White was left with a lasting impression: "He was intimidating."

Said younger brother Carlos, who played at Central and graduated in 1972: "He was mean on the court—he didn't take no crap."

He dominated inside, which was not a surprise. He dunked with authority, until it was outlawed prior to his senior year. He used a variety of spins and turnarounds, to both sides. His inside shots, which included an occasional skyhook, found the backboard or rim with a soft agreeable touch. His scoring average was in the low twenties only because he shot less frequently than urged to by his coach, Marquiss.

On defense and on the boards he channeled Bill Russell, the Boston Celtics player-coach. He was aggressive, he could leap, and he knew how to position. Dillard blocked four to six shots per game as a junior, and his zealous presence influenced the trajectory of untold others. He averaged more than twenty rebounds per game, and topped out at thirty-one, then a city record.

The surprise was his adept play outside the paint and at the perimeter. Dillard dribbled as well as smaller players, a skill he exploited on Central's fast break. He had an eye for the open man and often passed up a shot to assist a teammate's basket. When he shot from the ten-to-twenty-foot range, with a supple grooved stroke, the ball spun delicately off his fingertips. Had he come along thirty years later he might have been a number two guard at a major college.

"He was really ahead of his time for a guy his size," recalled Roy Hunter, a teammate.

But as good as Dillard was, he could have been better, and his teammates knew it. His attention wandered, he was distracted, and he often was less than serious. He smoked cigarettes despite their drain on his stamina, and he drank. Possibly basketball came too easily for him.

"He really didn't push himself along," recalled Griffin. "He was more of a natural athlete—his mind was on other things in his spare time."

As with most teenagers, Dillard had one foot in youth and one in manhood. Sometimes one was in his mouth.

After one game, Coach Marquiss treated the team at King's Food Host, where orders were phoned in from the booths. To keep a rein on the budget, the coach ordered for everybody. When the food arrived the hungry players dug in, except Dillard, who got on the phone, and said, "I'll have a bowl of soup." The order echoed over the restaurant's loudspeaker, which cracked up Dillard's teammates even as it infuriated Marquiss.

Dillard invented a comic expression in which his lips mimicked the motion of a fish under water, while his index finger and thumb cupped his chin. His bookkeeping teacher, Linda Ruecker, was an unwitting dupe. "He would ask her a question," recalled Howie Halperin. "She'd have her head down and he would turn to the class and do it. It was hilarious." Dillard's expression, copied by other students, became a standard gag in the hallways and cafeterias.

Anything was fair game for a laugh.

"He told one of the guys on the team he got a hard-on while he was up in front of a class," recalled Jeff Krum, a teammate. "This guy didn't know if Dwaine was putting him on or not but he said the way Dwaine described it was funny as hell."

Phyllis Mitchell was on her way to class when she was swept off her feet, literally, and deposited in a trashcan. Dillard, Willie Frazier, and John Biddle shook with laughter.

"It was one of those tall ones," she recalled. "I couldn't get out."

Anybody outside of Dillard's clique of friends might be the butt of his jokes.

Darryl Eure, a wrestler and track athlete, recalled that Dillard liked to knock—hard enough to hurt—on the heads of smaller students.

"Like you see in the kids' movies," Eure recalled. "He could be a knucklehead—both wonderful and irritating."

Occasionally Dillard became the butt of his own joke.

Curt Melton, a football player, had showered after practice when Dillard sized him up with a loud proclamation.

"You must be the skinniest guy on the football team."

As the laughter died down, Melton shot back, "You must be the skinniest guy on the basketball team."

The rejoinder surprised Dillard, who thereafter kept his distance, Melton recalled.

He liked to roam the locker room naked, snap a towel, and sting the buttocks of unsuspecting teammates. Once, he chose the wrong quarry, Alvin Mitchell, who was small, taciturn, and street tough. In an instant, Mitchell bounced three punches off Dillard's face.

"Dwaine went down—he didn't know what hit him," recalled Harvey Josin, a teammate. "The locker room was in an uproar."

He was ribald, caustic, and generous to a fault. He literally gave friends the sweater off his back. His prized white letter sweater was a gift from his mother, who had scrimped to buy it. But Dillard had not worn it for weeks, and she asked him why.

"One of the other guys wanted to wear it."

An audible wince accompanied her recollection.

"I wanted to hang him," Briggs recalled. "Back then money really was tight."

Dillard had a manic zest for horseplay with his pals, and for parties, music, and clothes. He liked the action on North Twenty-fourth Street, the gritty spine of the black neighborhood, and he liked the blue-collar feel of the South Side, his childhood neighborhood. He enjoyed the more genteel action in Bagel, to the west, the affluent neighborhood of his Jewish classmates. Mostly he liked girls, white and black equally, as long as they had a pulse.

"Before he'd go out he'd put on cologne—Jade East, Hai Karate—and stink out the house," recalled Carlos. "He wore starched collars and straight-legged pants."

"Willie Frazier would pick him up and Dwaine would say, 'We're going out to get the girls. One day you can be like us.'"

As Dillard's mother recalled, he had little difficulty finding female companionship—usually it found him.

"They kind of went after him—I don't think he fought them off," recalled Briggs. "I would come home from work and find slippers all around the house—like wild animals around a garbage can."

One evening, Central's assistant principal, Gaylord Moller, called to tell her that a father was upset that his daughter was seeing Dillard.

"That girl is over to my apartment now, and Dwaine didn't bring her here," Briggs told Moller.

The girl, who was white, had driven her father's motorcycle over to visit Dillard, and it had broken down outside Briggs's apartment. The father, who had complained to Moller, came to fetch his motorcycle.

"Dwaine was really friendly and if you weren't careful you could get caught up thinking that friendship meant more than it did," said Jawanda Gauff, a childhood friend.

One girl enamored of Dillard was Vikki Dollis, who alluded to Dillard's charm in the March 1, 1967, entry in her diary:

Today was the day 100 years ago Nebraska was admitted as a state. Thus it is our centennial. But that isn't what was important to me. The district tournament for state basketball champion started tonite. Although Central didn't play, Vicki's big sister, Cindy [Everson], and another varsity cheerleader, Marla West, took us out to see the game. Also some of our team (including Dwaine) were at the game and we all sat together. I've never had so much fun! All of our colored basketball players are such a riot; and after the game we were jacking around and they followed us to McDonald's to get something to eat. When we got there about five of them jumped in the car with us, and Dwaine was sitting next to me! He's so sweet to talk to, and when they left he kissed me on the cheek! I just love him and all the rest of the guys too! Cindy and Vicki and I were talking about how much fun the Negroes are on the way home, and it makes me wonder how anyone could ever be prejudiced. I could never be!

Throughout this adventuresome period, Dillard had a steady African American girlfriend, Barbara Essex, who was a year behind him at Central.

Dillard and Essex had dated since his sophomore year, and they were together at house parties, at north side YMCA events, or the latest film at the Beacon Theater on Ames Avenue.

She had been attracted to Dillard because he was handsome and fun, Essex recalled. She was proud to be Dillard's girl. But

Dwaine Dillard as a junior was "the best Central has ever seen." Photo courtesy of Carlos Dillard.

as time went on, and he became more of "a ladies' man," she became disenchanted. Though he continued to tell her she was special, she felt less so. And, as more time passed, she saw Dillard begin his lifelong struggle with alcohol.

When Dillard drank, recalled Essex, "he got ugly."

The product of a stable and comfortable upbringing, her father a porter for the Union Pacific Railroad, and her mother a caterer at Methodist Hospital, Essex found herself in a relationship that bore little resemblance to that of her parents.

"He would fight and bully," she recalled.

Her window into Dillard's soul and psyche provided a clouded—and sympathetic—view. Behind the bravado, laughter, and cruelty were the tears of a clown. All of the jokes, newspaper clips, applause, and hero worship could not dull the ache of a son abandoned by a father.

In March 1967 the *Omaha World-Herald* named him as the sole junior to its All-Metro team and wrote that he "may become Omaha's greatest schoolboy rebounder" and that he "has the college crowd in a sweaty-palm state." Central's 1966–67 team, with Ben Brown, Alvin Mitchell, Mark Wilson, and Willie Frazier, won its first fifteen games and was ranked number one in the state for most of the season.

But Dillard's junior year ended with a loss in the state final, to Lincoln Northeast, 64–57. Dillard was outplayed by Northeast's beefy center, Wally Winter, and scored just thirteen points before he fouled out.

The loss, perhaps, accounted for the modest tone with which he signed the *O-Book* — the school yearbook — of a classmate, Nancy Welchert: "It has been fun playing basketball this year and I hope to play next year also."

3

Summer of '67

Warren Marquiss smoked Lucky Strikes, lots of them. The smoke from his Luckies curled around his thin lips and high forehead and rendered him a whiter shade of pale. He liked to smoke in a dark equipment room with an iron-grill door known as "the cage," which abutted the gym at Central. The more nervous he was the more he smoked, and now, as he faced a career decision, his nerves were active.

Often, Marquiss motioned for Jim Martin, the junior varsity coach, to join him in the cage. Though Martin did not smoke, Marquiss liked his company, and they chatted about business, politics, and sports. During the season Marquiss's retreat to the cage usually signaled the end of practice.

"When Warren had to have a smoke he was done for the evening," recalled Martin.

But on this afternoon, in the spring of 1967, basketball season was over, and Marquiss had something to tell Martin.

"I'm stepping down," Marquiss said. "The job is yours."

Marquiss did not explain why, but Martin thought he knew—the runner-up finish in March 1967 had sapped his confidence. Martin wanted the head job, but he thought Marquiss would regret walking away from Dillard, and he thought Dillard would resent it.

Warren Marquiss—head coach and father figure. Photo courtesy of Carlos Dillard.

"I think you should stay," Martin told him.

"Why?"

"It's going to be awfully hard for me to step in with this group of kids," Martin said. "There's a lot of talent and it needs to be well-directed."

"You can handle it," Marquiss said.

"You've got a special gift for handling kids," Martin said. "You'll do fine."

"Dwaine trusts you."

The latter caught Marquiss's attention. To an extent, Dillard had chosen Central because of Marquiss, and had been vindicated. Marquiss had handled him with the right touch, at least in Dillard's view. The two were respectful, and even affectionate, toward one another.

Marquiss understood in his gut how Dillard might feel. His father, Charles Marquiss, of French descent, was a rogue. As Warren entered his teens, in the early 1930s, his father went to Colorado to race greyhounds and gamble, and stayed. Left behind were Warren, an older brother, and their mother, in a house on the rural northwestern edge of Omaha.

As the Depression deepened the family struggled. Marquiss's mother, Della, worked when she could, and she planted vegetable gardens and fruit trees, which the Marquiss boys tended when they came home from school. As little as she had, Marquiss's mother lodged indigents in her basement, for several years. She found solace in the New Deal of President Franklin Roosevelt, whose compassion for working people and the poor made an impression on her youngest son.

At Benson High Marquiss lettered in three sports but what he took from it, as he later told his sons, was that "my father never saw one of my games."

As a father Marquiss was all that his father was not. He taught his four sons to box and wrestle, coached their Little League baseball teams, and allowed them to tag along to his basketball games. He taught them to fish and hunt, and to share his appreciation for the outdoors. He worked a second job in the summers, as a real estate salesman, and he demanded an equal work ethic of his children. He was strict, but fair. "If you were told to do something you did it," recalled Don, his youngest son.

Marquiss's sons, and father, were among his thoughts as he deliberated another season as coach, and worried about Dillard. In the summer of '67 the Near North Side was relatively calm and Dillard stayed out of trouble. This wasn't a given, because now he was a star, and wherever he went he was fawned over. He frequented eateries, clubs, and pool halls on the North Side—Beverly Blackburn's, Chappie's Corner, Skeets—and at least one notorious dive—Lightning's—on the south side.

Lightning's, at Twenty-eighth and Q streets, operated between 9:00 p.m. and 4:00 a.m. and featured food, music, gambling, and prostitutes.

"It was a place where people got shot—people our age," recalled Delmar Givehand. "Dwaine went to gamble. A lot of us gambled but Dwaine really liked to gamble."

A block up the street was the Workman Club, another Dillard haunt, with a dance floor and live music on weekends. Across from the Workman was a corner lot with five upright pillars, known as Cadillac Square, so called because it was where pimps parked their cars. Dillard liked to kibbutz at Cadillac Square.

In the summer of '67, baby-boom Americans under eighteen peaked at seventy million, and young people dominated mass culture. A music festival at Monterey, California, made icons of Jimi Hendrix and Janis Joplin. The Beatles released *Sergeant Pepper's Lonely Hearts Club Band*, later judged by *Rolling Stone* magazine to be "the most important rock and roll album ever made . . . rock's greatest declaration of change." This was the "Summer of Love" in San Francisco, where the hippie movement reached its apogee of drugs, sex, and rock and roll. For Vikki Dollis, almost sixteen, it was a summer to search for

Vikki Dollis searched for love and kept a diary. Reprinted with permission of the *Omaha Central High School O-Book.*

love with one of Dillard's teammates, Jeff Krum, and within herself, as detailed in her diary for Tuesday, June 27:

I have so many emotions about this summer and I haven't really decided how I'll react to all of them. Cheerleading is an ever-increasing problem because the girls on Jr. Varsity hate the Varsity and all they do is talk about us all the time. And I fear that if I don't start taking summer school more seriously and start studying I'll fail the course. The same goes for Driver's Ed. And now with Sr. Lifesaving starting every night at 9:00 to 10 I don't know when I'll have time to study or sleep! Even my love life is confusing. Jeff Krum finally asked me out for Friday. Do I like him? Who knows?

Over the next month Dollis wrote about her feelings for Krum—uncertain; her body image—too heavy and muscular; her new hair style—short and "non-conformist"; and her cheerleading peers, from whom she felt ostracized because they considered her "stuck up and conceited."

Teen angst was augmented by public turmoil. In the inner cities of Detroit, Newark, and scores of others it was the summer of Molotov cocktails and "burn, baby, burn." Detroit counted forty-three dead and Newark twenty-three, as hundreds were injured and jailed. The cumulative toll from Detroit and Newark was less than the weekly casualty report from Vietnam, at the end of July, which listed 164 Americans killed and 1,442 wounded.

In Washington, President Lyndon Baines Johnson ordered another 55,000 troops to Vietnam, for a force that would reach 525,000, as total American casualties reached 12,269 dead and 74,818 wounded. "The tragedy is that we are today engaged in two wars and we are losing both," Dr. Martin Luther King Jr. said. "We are losing the war against poverty here at home. We are losing the war in Vietnam morally and politically."

In Montgomery, Alabama, it was the summer George C. Wallace raked in thousands of dollars of kickbacks from state contractors. Forced from office by term limits, the former governor, whose wife, Lurleen, succeeded him, stuffed the ill-gotten money into an account to fund a run for the presidency in 1968. Wallace had his eye on conservative white voters who held hippies and black rioters in equal contempt. He figured that each TV report of a "love-in" and a firebombed building increased his base of support.

George C. Wallace — "segregation forever." Reprinted with permission from the *Omaha World-Herald*.

Nobody in Omaha yet knew it — not Marquiss or Dillard — but Wallace was to enter their lives in a most unexpected way. To most Nebraskans, Alabama was a gothic backwater with which they had little contact, save for bitter defeats suffered in post-season football — Bear Bryant's all-white Crimson Tide over Bob Devaney's Cornhuskers — early in 1966 and 1967. That was about to change, due to Wallace.

The son of a poor dirt farmer, reared in a cracker-box house, diminutive, at five feet seven inches, Wallace's ambition was described as "messianic." In his youth he was an amateur boxing champion, a debater, and student leader at the University of Alabama Law School. He joined the Army Air Corps in

1942, served as a flight engineer on a B-29, and was in combat in the South Pacific.

At twenty-seven he was elected to the Alabama House of Representatives, served two terms, and pushed so-called do-gooder measures that helped servicemen and city and county employees. In 1953, at the age of thirty-four, he was elected to the Alabama judiciary and began to appear in Washington to testify against civil rights bills. He was an active member of the Democratic Party, and in 1958 he ran for governor. He was moderate on the issue of school segregation, lost by sixty-five thousand votes, and told other politicians, "John Patterson out-nigguhed me. And boys, I'm not goin' to be out-nigguhed again." He ran again in 1962, when Alabama's segregated schools were under attack by the U.S. Attorney's office, vowed to place his body in the door of any schoolhouse ordered to integrate, and was elected by a wide margin.

In his inaugural speech, Wallace pledged "segregation now, segregation tomorrow, segregation forever." In June 1963, with state troopers behind him, Wallace stood in the doorway of the University of Alabama's Foster Auditorium and refused entry to two black students, James Hood and Vivian Malone, who came to enroll. The Alabama National Guard intervened, and Wallace stood aside as the two youths registered.

The incident raised his national profile, and he began to speak on college campuses across the country. In 1964 he entered presidential primaries in Wisconsin, Indiana, and Maryland, tallied 30 percent or more in each state, but was marginalized by the political, religious, and media mainstream. In 1965 he sent state troopers to Selma, Alabama, where they helped local police batter and bloody civil rights advocates who had set out on a protest march to Montgomery. Forced by state law to relinquish the governor's office in 1966, Wallace put up his wife, Lurleen, as a proxy candidate, and won handily. In 1967 he conceived the American Independent Party with a state-rights anti-desegregation platform.

Now Wallace laid the groundwork for a third-party candidacy that played on the class and cultural resentment of those who shared his view that the national Democratic and Republican parties were "Tweedledee and Tweedledum."

Opposite Wallace on the political spectrum, in the summer of '67, the black power movement took root in sports—a movement that could not have escaped the attention of Dillard or any black high school athlete.

Perhaps the most notable act of rebellion was heavyweight champion Muhammad Ali's refusal, on religious grounds, to be inducted into the U.S. Army. Indicted in May on a federal felony offense, he was convicted on June 20 by a jury and sentenced to the maximum allowable five years in prison. His heavyweight title stripped, Ali became a martyr for both the black power and antiwar movements.

"He rebelled at a time when he, as an athlete, stood alone," wrote Harry Edwards, a black associate professor of sociology at San Jose State College. "He lost almost everything of value to any athlete—his prestige, his income, and his title. But he maintained and enhanced the most crucial factor in the minds of black people everywhere—black dignity."

Harry Edwards was a six-foot-eight former college basketball and track star with a noble, and activist, vision for black athletes. Soon Edwards launched what became known as the "Revolt of the Black Athlete" and drew inspiration from Ali and Bill Russell, who a year earlier had become player-coach of the Boston Celtics, and was the only black coach at the highest level of the pros. Russell, in his 1966 autobiography, had condemned racism in sports.

Edwards wrote that

the revolt of the black athlete in America as a phase of the overall black liberation movement is as legitimate as the sit-ins, the freedom rides, or any other manifestation of Afro-American efforts to gain freedom. . . . It was inevitable that this revolt should develop. With struggles being waged by black people in the areas of education, housing, employment and many others, it was only a matter of time before Afro-American athletes, too, shed their fantasies and delusions and asserted their manhood . . . at long last, the black athlete has entered the arena as a warrior in the struggle for black dignity and freedom.

The activist perception advanced by Edwards—as later described in Jack Olsen's June 1968 series in *Sports Illustrated*, "The Black Athlete: A Shameful Story"—was that black athletes at all levels of sport were exploited and were "dissatisfied, disgruntled, and disillusioned."

Black professional athletes, Olsen wrote, "say they are underpaid, shunted into certain stereotyped positions and treated like subhumans by Paleolithic coaches who regard them as watermelon-eating idiots."

Black college athletes were marginalized in campus social life and pressured to maintain athletic eligibility with light course loads that left them short of graduation—and unprepared for nonsports careers—when their eligibility ran out. In 1966 the University of Texas–El Paso (then Texas Western) was the first team to win the national college basketball championship with an all-black starting five—none of whom graduated.

Quoted in Olsen's series was George McCarty, the athletic director at Texas–El Paso: "In general, the nigger athlete is a little hungrier, and we have been blessed with having some real outstanding ones. We think they've done a lot for us, and we think we've done a lot for them."

Black high school athletes, Olsen wrote, often came from broken homes and poverty, and were encouraged to compete despite academic needs that went unaddressed. He profiled a black teenager, Robert Buford, at Kansas City's Lincoln High, who often went hungry.

Buford said:

When I'm gonna play in a game or run in a track meet, I try to always get lunch. I have to bum money—ask people to give me a nickel or a dime—and most of the time I don't eat. I never eat breakfast, and sometimes I miss the lunch meal and evening meal, too. I used to starve a lot . . . I was always sick, but I never showed it. I would try not to run lazy so they wouldn't know nothing was wrong.

Buford's father, who beat him as a young child, lived in Omaha while his mother, whom he had not seen in five years, lived with a man who beat her. Before he excelled in football, Buford was passed around by various relatives and finally slept in cars. Then his coach found him a part-time job, and he rented a one-room apartment with a stove and refrigerator. Buford told Olsen:

The people in my family were surprised that I kept on going to school after they put me out of the house. They thought I was

going to do like my brother and quit school and hang out in the
streets . . . ever since I was small, when I first went out for sports,
my people has always been throwing things and hitting me and
beating me, saying that I'm lying that I stayed out late because of
practice, that I was just hanging out in the street. When I tried to
tell them, they never listened. So when I got good at sports, then
they kind of brag on me, and that is what I hate.

Olsen wrote that Buford could barely read and write. But Buford would attend college because "he represents too great a temptation to certain American schools that are selling themselves to the public on the basis of their athletic reputations. . . . With his woodworking credits and his slow reading speed and his near inability to write, (he) is more than likely to wind up on a tree-lined campus, posing as Joe College."

So it was for Dillard. In the second semester of his junior year, he had failed General English and had passed American History, American Government, and Economics with a four, one grade above failure. His highest grade had been a three in Technical Drawing.

Before the end of the summer of 1967, Harry Edwards's group, United Black Students for Action, would force the cancellation of San Jose State's season-opening football game against Texas–El Paso, in protest of housing bias. Shortly thereafter the group transformed itself into the Olympic Project for Human Rights, which set out to organize a boycott of the 1968 Summer Olympics.

And back in Omaha, a couple of high-profile black athletes embodied the spirit of revolt. That summer Marlin Briscoe (South High School class of '63) prepared for his senior season as quarterback at Omaha University. Briscoe, who grew up in

the South Side projects as one of Dillard's role models, wanted
to play pro football, as a quarterback. But to do so required
a leap of faith; no black had held the quarterback position at
the highest level of pro football in its modern era, due to a
stereotype.

"For one reason or another, the American Negro athlete
is not primarily a thrower," Charles Maher wrote in the *Los
Angeles Times*.

*In baseball, there are few American Negro pitchers. In track and
field there are few Negro javelin throws, few Negro discus throwers, few Negro hammer throwers, few Negro shot-putters. And,
in pro football, there are no Negro quarterbacks. . . . Answering
the quarterback question, some football people said the Negro's
talents are such that he is more useful at other positions. Others
said the Negro has not shown that he can pass well enough. Still
others said that the Negro has not really been given a chance to
prove himself at this important leadership position.*

Briscoe knew what he was up against. "I was aware that being both black and small for a quarterback might work against
me," Briscoe wrote in his autobiography. "But I had refuted the
naysayers from midget football through college, so I started
to think I could make it in the pros and overcome those stereotypes again." He determined to showcase his skills one
more season at Omaha University, and to somehow make it
as a pro quarterback.

Meanwhile, in June, Bob Boozer (Tech High class of '55),
a member of the 1960 U.S. Olympic team, an eight-year NBA
veteran and captain of the Chicago Bulls, was rebuffed in his
effort to buy a residential lot in the northwest part of the city.

The developer cited racial bias and claimed that in a poll of property owners in the new subdivision, 30 percent "strongly objected" to Boozer's purchase and had threatened "to wreck" the development if he moved in.

"How do they have the right to sit on their fat mortgages and dictate whether I can move into this neighborhood?" Boozer told the media.

Boozer had returned to Omaha to take an off-season executive position with the telephone company.

"I was hoping to be judged as an individual and accepted on my own merits," Boozer said, "But apparently some Omahans cannot see beyond my color."

Boozer's experience reinforced a prime tenet of Edwards's "revolt"—that black athletes were welcomed by whites only in the arena and on the playing field, and that after the games ended, they were treated no differently than nonathlete blacks.

Three days before Boozer went public, the Nebraska legislature voted down a measure that would have banned housing discrimination. The measure would have negated restrictive laws passed in the 1920s that had kept blacks out of white neighborhoods.

Both events caught Marquiss's attention. Not only did he live in the part of the city where Boozer had tried to buy, he was a part-time real estate salesman.

The Boozer incident offended Marquiss. Since being hired at Central in 1947, and being named basketball coach in 1949, he had tried to be sensitive to the needs of his black athletes. He once noticed that photographers shied away from shooting them for feature stories. When he asked why, he was told they didn't show up as well in black-and-white photos.

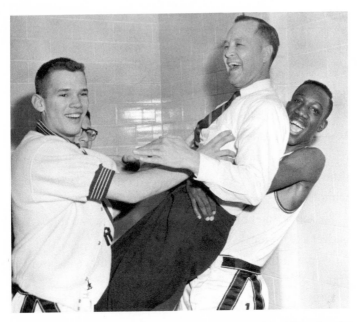

Steve Regelean (*left*), Coach Marquiss, and Walt Haney *right*) celebrate in 1963. Reprinted with permission of the *Omaha World-Herald*.

"If they rub oil on their skin will they photograph better?" Marquiss asked.

"Yes."

"That's what they'll do then."

Raised as a devout Protestant, Marquiss had a quiet, do-gooder Quaker aspect. For his poorest black players, he bought collared shirts, ties, slacks, and sport coats, so that they could meet his dress code. The money came from his own modest salary, as it did when he bought their families a bag of groceries.

Marquiss once delivered clothes and food to a player whose house had a dirt floor covered by cardboard. When he went home that evening, he told his sons, "You don't know how lucky you've got it."

Basketball, he believed, was the best chance for some of his players to go to college and escape the cycle of poverty. In this, he found himself at odds with the principal, J. Arthur Nelson, who disdained athletics and refused to fund them at the level Marquiss requested. Nelson made periodic and half-hearted requests for an upgrade to Central's obsolete facilities, at a time when newer schools had spacious gyms, and some older schools were enlarging.

Nelson was penurious about smaller items, and refused to budget a team meal after games in Lincoln.

"Some of these kids don't get a decent dinner," Marquiss argued.

"Get your alumni to pay for it," Nelson said.

Somehow, Marquiss found money for team meals, too often in his own pocket.

Money was a problem for Dillard, too, but less so in the summer of '67. He, Willie Frazier, and John Biddle were paid as part-time staffers at the new Bryant Basketball Center on North Twenty-fourth Street. The center, with four lighted outdoor courts, had opened in September 1966 as a response to the riot, the idea being that youths that had rioted, such as Dillard, needed recreational options.

Built on land donated by St. Benedict the Moor Parish, it was conceived by Rev. John J. Killoren, a Jesuit pastor with a progressive social vision, and named for George Bryant, the director of summer programs for the Department of Parks and Recreation. Federal grants funded a director, former Central star John Nared (class of '60), who hired the staff. Boozer was cochairman of the advisory committee.

Summer league games were played between 7:00 p.m. and 11:00 p.m., and sometimes until midnight. Central's core group of seniors—Dillard, Biddle, Frazier, Roy Hunter, Phil Griffin, Steve Moss, Ralph Hackney—and several reserves, comprised a team. Teams included players from Tech and North, the other high schools that drew from the North Side. Other teams had older players, some with college experience. Most of the players were black, except for those from Creighton Prep, the private and prestigious Jesuit school to the west, on Seventy-second Street.

The Prep players—Mike Peterson, Mark Langer, Dan Crnkovich, Bob Matthews, and Jim Haller—were there for the same reason as their Central counterparts, to prepare for the high school season. Prep's players were under the watchful eye of Brother Mike Wilmot, a Bryant supervisor who was Prep's assistant coach.

No statistics survive of the presumptive Central-Prep summer game, but Central won handily. The game provided an early glimpse of a regular season game that, several months later, would rivet the state and inspire a nickname.

"We could see we had something unique," recalled Roy Hunter.

By the time school resumed in September, Martin's persuasion and Dillard's presence prevailed. Marquiss returned for his nineteenth season as head coach of the Eagles. Nobody was more pleased than Dillard.

"He was a father to all of us—a great father image," Dillard recalled. "To me especially, because I had no father image."

4

Just Their Imagination

Basketball practice began just before Thanksgiving, about the time Vikki Dollis and Willie Frazier fell in love.

Frazier, a senior, at six feet one and a half inches, had been a starter at power forward the prior season and also had started at quarterback on the football team for most of two seasons. Strong and aggressive, Frazier outmuscled larger opponents inside and was not reticent about launching a twenty- to twenty-five-footer, with mixed success. Off the court, his shy smile, lilting voice, and sweet manner melted girls, and plunged him into romantic drama. He had dated another white girl, Sue Glyn, for more than a year when he began to see Dollis.

Dollis was hard to ignore, Central's version of the "It" girl, with brains to match her looks. Outwardly she appeared to have all the status and popularity a high school girl could want. But Dollis, like Dillard, had an invisible ache. She began to explore it through a biracial relationship, fraught with social angst.

Just six months earlier, it had been illegal for blacks and whites to marry in seventeen states in the South and Midwest. When the U.S. Supreme Court struck down Virginia's "anti-miscegenation" law, in June 1967, Maryland quickly repealed its law, and fifteen other state laws were rendered obsolete.

(Alabama was the last state to officially repeal its law, in 2000, though 40 percent voted to retain it.) Biracial couples now were free to marry in any state, if they could withstand the social pressures, as mocked in the Oscar-nominated film *Guess Who's Coming to Dinner?*

In a series of diary entries, Dollis described the joy and anguish of teen love across the racial divide. After she learned of Frazier's interest in her, she wrote:

Wednesday, November 29. My mind has rarely been in a turmoil as confused as it is now. My thoughts are completely disorganized and I have nowhere to turn for relief. That's why I spill out my troubles to you [diary] in hopes that they arrange themselves in some logical and comprehendable form. . . . The one fact that stands out in my mind is that I like Willie Frazier. The fact that he called me tonite and told me he liked me makes me extremely happy. But why do I like him? It is the same reason I would like any white boy. He intrigues me, and it would be a constant challenge to make us a very happy couple. For one second I forgot this earth and its people and their society and my only thoughts are of how attractive Willie is to me, and what it would be like to kiss him and love him and be with him like there was nothing wrong with it . . . what I can't understand is how so many people can profess a belief in God and still be prejudiced enough to see a difference in men because of the color of their skin . . . but right now in order to openly admit liking someone of a different race, I would have to fight not only the world and society, but my own family and friends. . . . I will have to love Willie secretly.

Thursday, November 30. I couldn't wait to talk to him after school and give him a letter I wrote him. In the letter I tried to explain

Willie Frazier—power forward and heartthrob. Photo courtesy of
Carlos Dillard.

*that if I liked him it would have to be secretly between him and
me so that I couldn't lose my reputation. But he didn't understand
too well so I tried for about 45 minutes tonite to convince him on
the phone. I don't know if what I said got through or not, but I'm
scared to make the decision to like him or not. I can't influence
the feeling of liking him, but I have to decide whether or not to act
like it. I'm so confused—and no one can tell me what to do.*

*Saturday, December 2. I've really gotten myself in a crisis for real
now. I was playing with fire all along, and I didn't realize until
tonite that I'd get burned if I wasn't careful. If I didn't know Willie
liked me I would never have had to go through this mess. But now
I'm in just deep enough to start worrying about finding the top*

before I drown. In other words I don't know myself if liking him would be more right than wrong anymore.

Sunday, December 3. I guess I can't see it now, but the reason I like Willie so much is because I can't like him and I'm extremely fascinated by colored boys. At least that's what everyone tells me, and everyone can't be wrong. I was so upset and confused that I cried all day and finally I went to see our minister, Dr. Naylor, tonite. He says I should like Willie but it would be unwise to date him because then white boys wouldn't ask me out anymore. And he's right so I'll have to make myself not like him anymore. That's the whole problem. I know I can't so I want to all the more. Right now I feel like I can stop liking him and everything will be okay. But tomorrow when I see him I'll like him.

Monday, December 4. I'm sure glad I figured out a way that things had a chance between Willie and me. I may be fighting just for the principle of the thing, but unless I have a right and a chance to get to know Willie better, I won't know if it's worth liking him and trying to protect my reputation at the same time. As long as I keep how I feel about Willie between me and him (and very few others who won't let it out) I can go on dating white boys and keep up my reputation. It's very dangerous, but I'll still go to parties to see Willie and no one cares if he calls me. It's my decision to endanger myself because I like to play with fire because I never think I'll get burned. Hope I don't!

Monday, December 18. I hope someone reads this someday and can understand just what I'm going through. Lately I have had the most awful hatred for people who condemn me for liking Willie. In the first place I don't know why they think it's any of

Dollis (*third row, left*) fell for Frazier. *Clockwise from Dollis:* Janet Taylor, Carmen Orduna, Jo Wagner, Patty Sacrider, Vicki Everson, Emily Bergquist (*center*), and Frankie Weiner. Reprinted with permission of the *Omaha Central High School O-Book*.

their business to talk about who I like or why I like anyone. If I have to not like someone just because of the color of his skin, then I'm not being at all Christian or fair or right. Maybe the reason I persist in liking Willie is to prove I think I have the right to like him. But the fact still remains that the way he has treated me has made me want to battle the whole world and society to deserve to have his love.

Saturday, December 23. I feel so warm and wonderful and beautiful right now. It's 12:30 and I'm sitting in the living room writing by the light from our Christmas tree. I just got home from Debbie Blanton's party. All day I was so excited and I couldn't wait till tonite. I have to admit it was pretty dull for awhile even when Willie got there. No one danced all night except for a few slow songs and Willie and I danced all of those! For awhile I was even talking to Ben Brown and I thought I like him, but all it took was one slow dance and I knew who I loved. At the end I gave Willie his Christmas present which was a little book called "What Color Is Love?" and he read it and looked at me so sweet! Before he left he kissed me and said Merry Christmas and I am in heaven. I'll never forget tonite.

Meanwhile, Marquiss readied his team for the season. He probably knew nothing of Frazier and Dollis, and if he had he would have paid them no mind. Off the court, his concerns were about the Vietnam War, which looked less and less like the "good war" in which he had fought. Initially he had supported it, as had most World War II veterans. But by 1968 he questioned the carnage that increased by the day.

That had not been the case in 1943, when he graduated from the University of Nebraska, with a major in chemistry, and was commissioned as a first lieutenant in the navy. Though he signed up for chemical warfare, he shipped out as a chief gunnery officer in the Pacific, aboard the USS *Wasp*, and shot at Japanese kamikaze aircraft.

He found it harder to send his oldest son off to Vietnam. When Jim Marquiss received a draft notice, the family physician gave him a physical. The doctor, who had played under

As the Vietnam War escalated, Central's color guard stood tall. Reprinted with permission of the *Omaha Central High School O-Book*.

Marquiss at Central, recommended Jim for a medical defer-ment, and he was classified 4–F.

The reason?

"I had had asthma as a kid," Jim Marquiss recalled.

Warren Marquiss turned against the war, because as a child of the New Deal, he leaned left politically, in the direction of the antiwar movement. And on a more basic level, as a biology teacher, he valued life.

What did this mean to Central's basketball team? Maybe nothing. But for many Americans the decision to oppose the war, and to doubt a sitting president, brought a personal liberation. For whatever reason, Marquiss, in his final season, embraced change, as he refashioned himself as a coach, relaxed control, and opened himself to hoop improvisation.

His change acknowledged the talent at hand, but not only that. He may have sensed that these players required different treatment in a different time. And he may have decided on a new approach because his old one had come up short. Only he knew the depth of his desire to win a state championship, a prize that had eluded and frustrated him. As a chain-smoker, in a basketball sense, he was down to his last puff.

The season tipped off after Christmas with the traditional Holiday Tournament that included fourteen schools. The *World-Herald* ignored what had been foreshadowed at the Bryant Center and picked Creighton Prep as the favorite.

Indeed, Central stumbled at the outset. The squad struggled as Marquiss stewed over his starting five, a sensitive issue. Historically, at least one white player had started for Central. The lion-in-winter principal, Nelson, concerned about public image, preferred at least one white starter, and Marquiss always had managed to start one. (An all-black five is said to have started one game in 1957, when the white starter, Phil Barth, was injured.)

Whether Marquiss ever started a white player less talented and deserving than a black player is a matter of debate. Tim Schmad, the lone white starter on the 1963 team, did not believe race was involved in Marquiss's decision.

"Warren would have started whoever he needed to start," Schmad recalled.

Yet a perception lingered that talent wasn't the sole determinant. That year, Schmad's mother was president of the PTA—an organization dominated by white parents.

"I remember thinking, 'I hope they don't start me because she's PTA president,'" Schmad recalled.

In 1967 the same perception lingered, with a variation.

"He won't start five blacks," Phil Griffin, a senior, told a teammate. "The school board won't allow it."

Harvey Josin, a junior forward and one of the two white players, started the first game. Nerves got the better of Josin: he clanked a wide-open shot and committed three quick fouls. Soon enough, Griffin replaced him. With Griffin on the floor Marquiss saw the chemistry of an effective—and potentially dazzling—unit. Central rallied to win its opener, against Boys Town, by a point.

Griffin started the second game, and though it was a single-point loss to Tech, Marquiss liked what he saw. Griffin started the third game and soon it was clear that the "quota" system had died an overdue and well-deserved death. Nelson and certain alumni voiced their concerns to Marquiss, who held his ground. He told his starters to ignore comments and rumors they were bound to hear.

"I'm going with this," he told them, "and I'll deal with the heat."

Central's quiet change went unremarked in the local media, but not among black athletes at South High, where a perceived quota system still was observed. Black athletes at Tech and

North also would have noticed, said Hayden West, a childhood friend of Dillard's who was a junior on the South team.

"It was monumental, that someone had the guts to do this," recalled West.

Creighton Prep won the Holiday Tournament and got off to a stronger start. But Central began to jell as the other three starters—John Biddle, Roy Hunter, and Phil Griffin—blended with Dillard and Frazier.

John Biddle, a five-foot-eleven senior with the brawny build of a weight lifter, was the point guard, and unofficial captain. The eighth of nine children, Biddle brought a discipline to basketball acquired at his mother's bakery, where he had worked since the age of thirteen. The *Register* referred to Biddle as "the Magician," which described both his slick ball handling and playmaking skills, and his confident, composed, wink-at-you persona. An eager and motivated student, Biddle enjoyed his classes as much as basketball.

Roy Hunter, the off guard, was a senior who, at five feet ten and a half inches, his teammates liked to say, "could jump out of the gym." His vertical leap was so explosive he played as a guard-forward, and grabbed more rebounds and blocked more shots than most forwards. Hunter's older brother, Jim, had been an all-city forward in 1966, a prolific scorer, and Hunter suffered by the inevitable comparison. He did not shoot as well as his brother, one theory being that he jumped so high, and hung in the air so long, that he was off balance. But Hunter was so polite, soft-spoken, and shy that his thoughts and feelings—about almost everything—usually were kept to himself.

Phil Griffin, a six-foot-one senior with a quick first step and deft move to the bucket, was at weak forward. Of the five, he was the outsider, having transferred from South to Central as a junior. The last player named to the starting five, he was odd man out of the offense, at the start, but less so as the season progressed and confidence grew in his arching baseline jumper and his steady midrange game. The son of an Arkansas farmer who cleared a racial barrier to find work at one of Omaha's most prestigious manufacturers, Griffin had a country manner—laconic and droll. In face and physique, he was a fair copy of Satchel Paige, the legendary pitcher.

The bench consisted of Steve Moss, a senior guard; his brother, Jerry Moss, a junior guard; Ralph Hackney, a senior guard; Henry Caruthers, a junior guard; Phil Allison, a junior forward; Jeff Krum, a junior forward; Homer Lee Harris, a junior forward; and Harvey Josin.

At the outset Marquiss had acted on habit and installed the patterned double-post offense that was his trademark. Phil Barth, point guard on the 1958 team, recalled that Marquiss taught a handful of plays, which did not include a fast break.

"We had certain plays Warren always used—every team we played knew they were coming," Barth recalled.

Schmad described Marquiss as "analytical," a coach who identified scorers, ball-handlers, rebounders, and defenders, and plugged them into a predictable system.

"We ran the same plays in 1963 that he ran in 1953," recalled Schmad. "His theory was do it over and over and do it right."

So it was in 1968—for a short while. He taught his most basic play, "man down the middle," in which the point guard,

Biddle, passed off, broke down the lane, and veered toward a corner. "We'd set a screen a certain way, and the guy on the wing would break around and get to the corner, and usually be open," recalled Hunter.

Marquiss installed a fast break—that much had changed since 1958—to exploit Dillard's dominance on the boards, and insisted on an alert and aggressive transition, especially to defense.

"His feeling was that you got beat in the transition game," recalled his son, Don. "He believed you had to keep transition at both ends and get to those positions and fill the lanes."

Practices were no-nonsense, fast-paced replicas of game conditions. Ball movement and set patterns were emphasized.

"We knew where our spots were and what our limitations were," Biddle recalled. " It got to where it was like falling off a log."

By 1968 it was predictable—perhaps too much so. After the first game or two, Dillard told Marquiss he felt constrained by the double low post.

"Open it up," Dillard pleaded. "I can shoot from anywhere."

Marquiss thought it over and agreed. Dillard was allowed his freedom, and improvisation took root.

"We ran a three-two offense that people didn't realize," Hunter recalled. "Dwaine was the center but a lot of times he played as forward. You could set a screen and he would roll one way or the other way and be wide open. Or we would set a double screen and his guy couldn't get to him and there he was."

Th-th-th-that's all folks!

They held the world in their hands. *Clockwise from top*: Dwaine Dillard, John Biddle, Phil Griffin, Ralph Hackney, and Roy Hunter. Reprinted with permission of the *Omaha Central High School O-Book*.

That decision led to other new wrinkles—all of which gave his players more freedom. They began playing with imagination, running away with games. The fast break became more creative. The full-court press, popularized by UCLA under John Wooden, became more spontaneous. Biddle harassed the inbound pass, while Hunter, Frazier, and Griffin trapped the receiver. Dillard was quick enough to neutralize, and intercept, long outlet passes. Marquiss applied the press when he sensed an opponent was too comfortable in its half-court offense, but as often as not, the players applied it themselves. They could handle an up-tempo game; most opponents could not.

As Marquiss relaxed authority he dialed down the intensity of daily practice.

"He never raised his voice at practice—he let the players play," recalled Griffin. "He wouldn't get on your butt or prod you."

Other than an inbounds play and a formation for the press, Griffin recalled, Marquiss abandoned repetition and breakdown of set plays. Practice, for the most part, consisted of five-on-five competition. When Marquiss retreated to the "cage" for a cigarette, players shot free throws.

"The practices were laid back," recalled Jim Martin, the junior varsity coach.

With their third game, the Eagles began a winning streak that confirmed Marquiss's new approach. The streak included a 71–53 payback win over Omaha Tech, whose lineup included future Nebraska wingback and Heisman Trophy winner Johnny Rodgers, and All-Metro bruiser Ernie Britt. Central's 62–41 rebounding edge reflected the dominance of Dillard, for whom twenty or more boards was routine.

In a 63–51 win over Westside, Biddle scored fifteen including nine straight free throws. Against Lincoln High, the only team to defeat Creighton Prep, Central led by just 31–29 after three quarters. Dillard and Frazier each scored eight in the final quarter for a 50–35 win.

Off the court, Frazier's life became more complicated. He broke up with Dollis, offered no explanation, and brought her to tears and despair. A day later he stayed home from school and called Dollis in the evening to explain why he broke up with her: his former girlfriend, Sue Glyn, had told him she was pregnant by him.

"He doesn't know whether or not to believe her," Dollis wrote, "but if she is he will feel so bad he'd change schools and it would ruin him."

Glyn, with whom Frazier had a longtime relationship, indeed was pregnant. When she told him, "he dropped me," Glyn recalled.

Frazier's entanglements did not affect the team's performance. Thomas Jefferson High gave Central a scare, using a press to build a 26–18 halftime lead. Biddle broke the press in the second half and distributed to Dillard, Griffin, and Hunter, whose eleven points and ten rebounds were key to the 64–54 win.

Bellevue was done in, 86–39, by Central's fast break and a thirty-one-point effort by Dillard. Abraham Lincoln fell, 74–61, as Dillard notched thirty-four points, thirty rebounds, and ten blocked shots. His social life kept apace, as Dollis noted on February 2:

Tonite after the game Janie & Pam & Dinnie & Carmen & I did one of the stupidest things we've ever done. Dwaine & Ralph & Biddle & some of the other basketball players took 2 white girls over to Dwaine's house, so we followed them and they caught us spying on them! We all died of complete embarrassment and we'll never be able to face any of them again.

By this time Marquiss understood that he was more chaperone than coach. His job was to get the team to and from the game — the players would take care of the rest.

Less coaching proved to be more. Central ran its win streak to ten against Archbishop Rummel in a game that was less memorable for the outcome than for racial slurs hurled at Central players from the Rummel bleachers. Rummel attacked Dillard with an aggressive physical strategy, lured him into early fouls, and was tied at forty after three quarters.

"One player grabbed Dwaine around the neck — they were trying to get him to retaliate," recalled Hunter.

But Dillard kept his cool and controlled the boards in the final quarter while Frazier popped for nine of his nineteen points in a 60–49 win. The game was played at Rummel, located in a white working-class neighborhood in north central Omaha. The atmosphere was tense enough that Marquiss ordered his team to forego showers and head straight to the bus after the final whistle.

"They called us all kinds of things — I was shocked," recalled Hunter.

The Rummel neighborhood, known as Roncalli, "was notorious for its unreconstructed attitude," recalled Dan Daly. It was the type of neighborhood — fearful of a black incursion — targeted by George Wallace as he kicked off his presidential campaign early in January 1968. In California he declared that "the Supreme Court of our country has handcuffed police" and that the courts "turn people loose every day who are self-proven and confessed murderers of five or more people." Wallace promised to restore "law and order," a message coded with racial undertones that resounded in Roncalli.

As Dillard saw it, most of Omaha was not too much different from Roncalli, white and segregated. Black residents were confined to the Near North Side, or in a small area near the packinghouses in south Omaha where Dillard's mother lived.

Some of Central's opponents represented those segregated neighborhoods. Benson, an old school to the northwest, bordered Roncalli. Westside and Burke were new schools in the upscale western suburbs. Bryan was a new school in a south-central neighborhood. Creighton Prep, to the west, and Archbishop Ryan, to the southwest, were Catholic schools attended by few black students.

Indeed, Central's "home" games were played at Norris Junior High, because the bandbox gym at Central was too small and obsolete. Norris, just south of midtown, was in an older neighborhood, white and segregated, where Vikki Dollis and Sue Glyn lived.

One evening, as Dillard and Frazier arrived at Norris, Dillard was struck by a paradox.

"This is our home court," he said.

Frazier nodded.

"You see any black folks in this neighborhood?"

"Nope."

"Does it feel like home to you?"

"Nope."

"Me neither."

Two days after the Rummel game, Dillard and a female classmate were suspended for using "foul language" at school. The outburst—perhaps of anger and indignation—caused Dillard to miss three days of school and practice, but no games.

During this period Dillard attended a party at the upscale home of Danny Rubin in Bagel, the Jewish neighborhood to the west. The party—to celebrate Rubin's graduation, a semester late—featured a live band and attracted a crowd of about two hundred. Despite the presence of an off-duty Omaha cop, hired by Rubin's father, beer, malt liquor, and cheap wine were prevalent.

"Everybody gave Dwaine booze," Rubin recalled. "He went up to my bedroom and laid down on my bed. Then he got up and puked in the bathroom."

Four of Dillard's friends carried him out and got him home. By now drinking to excess had become the norm, which worried his girlfriend, Barbara Essex. She began to dread his drinking because it made him mean.

At Dillard's worst, Essex recalled, "he was aggressive, abusive."

When Dillard returned, the team did not lose its stride. Comfortable seven-point and twelve-point wins over Ryan and Boys Town brought the streak to twelve. Meanwhile, Creighton Prep had won ten straight.

A week before Central was to play Creighton Prep, sports columnist Wally Provost wrote, in jest, that the teams were "rushing toward a collision too horrible to contemplate." On a more sober note he wrote that Central fans had complained about Prep's number one ranking, and had cited "'bias' and 'prejudice' in keeping with the irascible nature of our suspicious, supersensitive times."

Five days before the showdown, the *World-Herald* leapfrogged Central over Prep in the rankings, based on comparative margins of victory. Now Central was number one and Prep was number two, but either way, fans were primed. Prep Coach Tom Brosnihan suggested publicly that if the game were played at the Civic Auditorium downtown, instead of at Norris Junior High, it could draw eight thousand spectators. But Marquiss clung to his home-court advantage and refused.

He sought another edge. Marquiss usually did not scout opponents, but for this game he made an exception. He had the second unit run Prep's offense in practice, so that the starters would know what to expect.

Two days before the game, Nebraska Secretary of State Frank Marsh placed George C. Wallace's name on the ballot for the Nebraska presidential primary on May 14. Wallace was entered as a Democrat, which was problematic. Nebraska Democrats did not want Wallace in their primary, and Wallace did not want to be in their primary. As America's foremost racist and segregationist, Wallace had his own party, the American Independent Party, but it had not met Nebraska's petition requirement to be listed on the primary ballot.

Wallace decided to petition Nebraska voters to get his third party on the ballot. His decision, at his headquarters in Montgomery, Alabama, occurred just a few hours before the Harry Edwards–organized boycott of the New York Athletic Club (NYAC) track meet, a rehearsal for the boycott of the 1968 Summer Olympics.

The NYAC was targeted because its membership did not allow blacks or Jews. The boycott, Edwards wrote, would "regain some of the dignity that black athletes had compromised . . . by participating for a club that would not even allow a black person to shower in its facilities."

Though the meet went off as scheduled, numerous black athletes, entire college teams, and the Russian national team pulled out, and attendance was off by 50 percent.

Edwards claimed a modest victory for the Revolt of the Black Athlete, even as five black athletes were desperate to get to a packed Omaha gym, in a neighborhood where they could play basketball, but not live.

5

So Glad They Made It

On the evening of Friday, February 16, Steve Moss's car broke down. The 1959 white Lincoln convertible coughed, sputtered, and stopped. His passengers groaned as he climbed out and raised the hood.

High school seniors drove old cars and breakdowns happened. But this breakdown was more than inconvenient. Moss's passengers were four of Central's starting five—Dillard, Biddle, Griffin, and Hunter. Moss himself was a top reserve.

While Moss fiddled under the hood, the gym at Norris Junior High thrummed at high idle. At 8:00 p.m., Nebraska's top-rated team, Central (13-1), would tip off against second-rated Creighton Prep (14-1). The 3,200-seat gym had filled up by 6:00 p.m., and the school auditorium held a spillover crowd of eight hundred for a closed-circuit telecast. Radio station WOW would broadcast the play-by-play to the rest of Omaha. Two *World-Herald* reporters, Paul LeBar and Don Lee, were in the stands. Prep fans unfurled a banner that ran the length of the bleachers: "Pour Central Down the Dwaine."

The prospect of being late for the most important game of the season paralyzed everyone, except for Dillard, who suggested his teammates get out and push.

"Yo' mama, too," someone said.

"No, yo' mama."

"Yo' mama's mama."

"She kick yo' ass."

Nervous laughter.

"Be cool," he assured his teammates.

They all but resolved to jog, or hitchhike, and to arrive late, when Moss got the engine to turn over. He put the pedal down and raced toward the junior high, a few miles away. They arrived twelve minutes before tip-off, and dashed into the locker room, where Marquiss nearly was apoplectic.

"We got changed and went onto the court without a warm-up," recalled Hunter.

The temperature of Central fans rose as the feet of the wayward five hit the floor. The Eagles entered on an emotional wave and stayed on it as the public-address announcer, English teacher Dan Daly, read the lineups. At the final note of the national anthem, Central senior Jerry Raznick shouted his ritualistic, "Dillard's hot!" and swiped "skin"—the forerunner of the high five—with classmate Howie Halperin.

At the tip-off both teams struggled. Two minutes elapsed before Frazier's ten-footer opened the scoring. Prep hit one of its first nine shots, while Central hit two of its first thirteen, and trailed after a quarter, 7–5. Absent the hoopla, spectators and media might have made an early exit. But they would have missed something definitive.

For the next eight minutes, then sixteen, then twenty-four, Central played basketball better than it had, or knew it could. The pace quickened, then slowed, and quickened again, to a beat only five could hear, but plenty could see—a syncopation of purple and white uniforms.

Central High 1967–68 varsity basketball: (*bottom row, left to right*) Willie Frazier, Ralph Hackney, Phil Griffin, Dwaine Dillard, John Biddle, Roy Hunter, Steve Moss; (*second row, left to right*) Henry Caruthers, Phil Allison, Steve Spurlock (junior varsity), Harvey Josin, Jeff Krum; (*top row, left to right*) Coach Warren Marquiss, Homer Lee Harris, Jerry Moss, Mike Sherman (manager), Bob Jacobson (manager). Reprinted with permission of the *Omaha Central High School O-Book*.

As Marquiss watched he could only have felt vindication in his prowess as a coach. Before him was proof of his new approach.

Creighton Prep, a good team, could not comprehend Central, at least on this night. Perhaps no high school team—anywhere—could have.

LeBar wrote that the second quarter was Central's "home-run stanza," an allusion to poetry, which was apt, and to baseball, which wasn't.

Statistics told a partial story. The Eagles hit eleven of thirteen shots, several on fast-break lay-ups, and moved from an 11–5 deficit to a 28–21 halftime lead. They hit five of six to start the third quarter and moved out to a 40–28 lead. Prep got no closer than 50–40 early in the fourth quarter.

Central won, 61–48. The starting five played all thirty-two minutes for the first time. Frazier scored twelve, held the taller

Dillard once grabbed thirty-one rebounds in a single game. Photo courtesy of Carlos Dillard.

Peterson to eighteen, and muscled him off the boards. Biddle scored eleven with a near-flawless floor game. Griffin had nine and Hunter six.

Dillard led all scorers with twenty-three, but it was his eighteen rebounds, and Central's 39–22 rebound edge that "made whatever Prep could do but a wasted gesture," LeBar wrote.

"They beat us—no alibis," said Brosnihan, Prep's coach.

This was more than a win for Central. It was a virtuoso. At its best, basketball is a game of tempo, rhythm, discipline, and instinct. Those things also describe the making of music, and in a figurative sense, that's what the five starters had done. They had turned basketball into art. They had made beautiful music.

Afterward, Don Lee asked Marquiss if this team was better than last season's state runner-up. Marquiss ducked the question, but his response revealed something more fundamental.

"That's like asking which of your kids you like best," Marquiss said.

Asked the same question, Dillard did not hesitate.

"Yes," he said. "Because of our teamwork and Mr. Marquiss, especially."

Then Lee, a twenty-five-year veteran of the high school beat, wrote his story. He had a knack for nicknames, as well as a grasp of basketball, and in his sidebar he achieved convergence.

Lee wrote: "It was a five-man victory, with the Rhythm Boys playing the entire 32 minutes. Willie Frazier, John Biddle, Phil Griffin, and Roy Hunter lined up behind the fabulous Dillard."

Thus the Rhythm Boys were born in print.

The moniker appeared again on February 18. The story, absent a byline, reaffirmed Central's number one ranking.

"Using only 'the Rhythm Boys' (starters), Central blasted Prep, 61–44, to bolster its position," it read.

Notwithstanding the incorrect score, the second use by the state's dominant newspaper reinforced the nickname. Though Don Lee was first to write it, whether he originated it is unclear. It may well have percolated up from the hallways of Central, or the team itself, and been transmitted to Lee via Marquiss. The two veterans had a professional relationship going back nineteen years.

A colleague of Lee's guessed that he coined it.

"If I had to bet one way or another I'd bet on his touch," said Conde Sargent, a sportswriter from 1963 to 1976. "He put more nicknames on athletes than any man in history. He turned a good halfback from Boys Town, Byron McCain, into Hurricane McCain. He slapped those little nicknames on almost every athlete he covered."

Some nicknames stick and some fade away, for reasons as mysterious as the ebb and flow of culture. This one stuck. Soon it was part of the lexicon of Central's student body and some of the players themselves. "John Biddle started calling the team the Rhythm Boys," recalled Bonnie Knight.

"One time Willie Frazier came over to the bench and said to Warren, 'Here come the Rhythm Boys,'" recalled Dan Daly. "They referred to themselves that way."

The nickname suited their chemistry. They shared a bond that went beyond the giving and receiving of skin. They referred to one another—with comic affection—by their mothers' names: Dillard was "Phyllis," Frazier was "Pearl," Biddle was "Sadie," and so on. They were comfortable together—the nickname said so.

Not everybody cared for the nickname. Darryl Eure and a number of his like-minded friends found it offensive. Later in

1968 Eure, whose mother was an early leader in Omaha's civil rights movement, would found a Central group called Black United Students of Soul (BUSS). Among its members would be six basketball players—Henry Caruthers, Phil Allison, Homer Lee Harris, Lindbergh White, John Lott, and Ken Secret—and several women—Debra Teamer, Bebra Flakyes, Shirley MacPhaull, Jo Ann Donaldson, and Patricia Value.

Eure lodged a complaint with the principal, J. Arthur Nelson.

"It's demeaning and stereotyped," he said.

Twenty-five years earlier, the nickname would have excited little concern; it might have described a black jazz orchestra led by Lloyd Hunter, Roy's uncle. Forty years earlier a white male singing trio, which included Bing Crosby, were known as the Rhythm Boys.

But in 1968 "the Rhythm Boys" straddled a fault line of American life. The fault line, which cut through race, politics, science, and the arts, groaned and creaked, zigged and zagged. Each day the ground moved underfoot, and people and institutions teetered.

Language and words teetered, too. "Negro," which had replaced "colored" in the civil rights lexicon, was under assault. The militant H. Rap Brown said, "Negro is a slave word," and insisted on the word "black." Surveys by newspapers and magazines showed that black readers preferred "Afro-American" or "black."

Black students such as Eure were drawn to a new breed of activist leaders and indifferent to Dr. Martin Luther King Jr., who continued to use "Negro," and whose gospel of nonviolence, it seemed, had fallen short.

In Oakland, California, the Black Panther Party, founded by Huey P. Newton and Bobby Seale, had sprung up in 1966 and asserted violence as an option in response to what they saw as widespread police brutality in their neighborhood. But early in 1968 the Omaha chapter, organized by Eddie Bolden, Veronza Bowers, and James Grigsby, was a few months from opening its door.

That left the activist field to thirty-year-old Ernie Chambers, a bearded and chiseled weightlifter, and a graduate of Creighton University School of Law, who had spoken at Central within the past year. An overflow crowd in room 215, the largest study hall, had heard Chambers revile the school department and white racism, and warn black students that whites—students, faculty, and administrators—were not to be trusted. At one point Chambers pointed at Moller, the assistant principal, at the back of the hall, and said, "That man is racist—he's not to be trusted."

Many black students, Dillard among them, needed no introduction to Chambers—he cut their hair at Dan Goodwin's Spencer Street Barbershop. He had been an articulate and forceful voice on the North Side since the early 1960s, and had seemed to become more militant in 1966 when he said, "Someone will have to blow up downtown Omaha to convince the white power structure that we mean business, that we are damn sick of imprisonment in this stinking ghetto."

Chambers's profile had gone national in 1966 with the airing of the documentary *A Time for Burning*. During filming, the Lutheran pastor, William Youngdahl, had sought a dialogue with Chambers at the barbershop. But Chambers, contemptu-

Ernie Chambers—militant barber. Reprinted with permission of the *Omaha World-Herald*.

ous and opportunistic, played to the camera and harangued Youngdahl with a litany of white transgressions, as the pastor's face beaded with sweat.

"You guys pull the strings that close schools . . . you throw the bombs that keep our kids restricted to the ghetto . . . you write up the restrictive covenants that keep us out of houses," Chambers said. "You're treaty breakers, liars, and thieves. You rape entire continents and then you wonder why these very people don't have any confidence or trust in you. Your religion means nothing—your laws are a farce—we see it every day . . . as far as we are concerned your Jesus is contaminated just like everything else you've tried to force upon us is contaminated."

Arms folded and eyes cast down, a study in contrition, Youngdahl listened until Chambers paused for a breath.

"I genuinely feel I want to listen," Youngdahl said.

"If you listen you'll get kicked out of your church—that's the way your people are," Chambers said.

As it turned out, Youngdahl was fired by church elders at the end of his first year. With that dead-on prophecy, Chambers's stature increased. Darryl Eure and the future members of BUSS were under the sway of Chambers, all the more when the Kerner Commission published its findings on February 29, 1968. Officially known as the National Advisory Commission on Civil Disorders, it was created by President Johnson to investigate the causes of inner-city riots.

The bombshell report led national and local news. Atop page 1 was the headline "Riot Panel Says Racism Could Split This Nation."

"Our nation is moving toward two societies, one black, one white—separate and unequal," the report stated.

It concluded that blacks were frustrated with lack of jobs, which was predictable, and white racism, which was not. The official finger pointed at whites validated what black activists had claimed for years. In essence, rioters are victims—don't blame them. Blame their environment and the institutions and attitudes responsible. The report proposed massive levels of government funding for new housing, education, job training, and welfare.

The report was built upon the testimony of black leaders, including Chambers, one of a select few who had testified be-

Ernie Chambers—"Black people have been systematically murdered by the government." Reprinted with permission of the *Omaha
Central High School O-Book*.

hind the committee's closed doors. Chambers testified that
nonwhites "have marched, cried, prayed, voted, petitioned,
and tried every possible way to make this white man recognize
us as human beings, and he refuses." With the Kerner Report,
the ground shifted.

Opposite Chambers, in a figurative sense, were Sidney Poitier
and mainstream Hollywood. Just four days after the Central-

Prep game, two of Poitier's films—*In the Heat of the Night*, a drama about race, and *Guess Who's Coming to Dinner?* a comedy about race—were nominated for Best Picture of 1967. Poitier played the black lead in both films. He starred in a third film, *To Sir, with Love*, that was a box-office hit in 1967.

Poitier, the highest-paid black actor of the day, played characters of deliberately typecast, reverse racial stereotypes. They were idealized characters that white viewers could admire—and feel themselves tolerant and open-minded.

But Poitier's role in *Heat* confounded his critics. He played a Philadelphia detective, Virgil Tibbs, who found himself in a small Mississippi town helping the white sheriff solve a murder. An electric moment occurred when Tibbs, in questioning a racist grandee, received a backhand hard to the face. In an instant he returned the backhand in kind, to the shock of the grandee. The scene elicited cheers from black viewers across America. Virgil Tibbs, with that slap, made the ground move.

Heat won the Oscar for Best Picture, even as the entertainment industry was put on notice by the Kerner Report, which concluded that network TV "must hire Negroes, it must show Negroes on the air, it must schedule programs relevant to the black ghetto."

Although the Kerner Report did not connect race to Vietnam, others did. As early as 1965 Chambers had voiced cynicism about American militarism in *A Time For Burning*.

"The white man tells you to bleed, you go bleed," Chambers had said. "He tells you to go to Korea and you go because you have to. He tells you to go to Vietnam or Lebanon or Laos and we have to go bleed.

"Then in Mississippi or Alabama or Omaha, Nebraska, where they're taking our rights and we know who's taking them we don't have any blood then. We fight overseas to defend his women and children and defend his line from attack, and while we're over there fighting for him our own people over here are being attacked by the same people we're fighting to defend."

But the two issues—race and Vietnam—were not joined for the public until February 1967 when King spoke out against the war, based on his belief that young black men were its disproportionate victims.

By January 1968 nearly sixteen thousand Americans had died, and more than one hundred thousand had been wounded. The number of U.S. troops in Vietnam stood at five hundred thousand.

Now, in February 1968, North Vietnamese forces and the Viet Cong unleashed the Tet Offensive. The massive coordinated attack throughout South Vietnam shocked the American public, which had been told repeatedly by Johnson that the war would be won. On February 18, just two days after the Central-Prep game, the United States posted its highest one-week casualty figures: 543 killed, 2,547 wounded.

With Tet, the ground shifted under the White House. Johnson's approval ratings fell from 63 percent to 47 percent in February. One month later, the percentage of Americans confident in the progress of the war fell from 74 to 54 percent.

The groundswell against Johnson, and Vietnam, crystallized in a Pete Seeger song, "Waist Deep in the Big Muddy." He sang it on the *Smothers Brothers Comedy Hour*, on February 25, 1968—five months after CBS management had censored his original appearance. The song is the story of a platoon on patrol wading in a river, driven by a reckless captain, until it is neck-deep in water. Each verse ends with the line "The big fool said to push on" — a barbed allusion to Johnson.

Two days later, venerable CBS news anchor Walter Cronkite sobered millions of viewers with an on-air opinion, "We have been too often disappointed by the optimism of the American leaders, both in Vietnam and Washington, to have faith any longer in the silver linings they find in the darkest clouds." Cronkite's comment further damaged Johnson.

All of this seemed distant from Central but it wasn't. Five Central graduates already had died in Vietnam, another would perish (James W. Fous) before the school year was out, and yet another four would die within two-and-a-half years, bringing the total to ten.

Soon the groaning and creaking that was America in 1968 would not seem distant at all, not from Central, and not from the Rhythm Boys.

Nebraska was one of just thirteen states with a primary election before the November presidential election. As Johnson's popularity plummeted in February, each primary grew in significance, including Nebraska's on May 14.

Among the candidates circling Johnson's carcass was Wallace, forty-eight, whose pugnacious face and slicked-back hair had become familiar to most Americans.

Typical of Wallace was his reaction to the Kerner Report. He found it "unbelievable" that the panel "apologizes for those who break down law and order." Inner-city riots were not the result of white racism, Wallace insisted, but of the actions of "militant activists, Communists, anarchists, and revolutionists."

"Those who have instigated the breakdown of law and order are the same ones who wind up in a North Peking and Moscow the next week," he said.

As for Vietnam, college professors and students who advocate for a withdrawal without victory, he said, should be "drawn by the hair of the head . . . to a good jail." To European allies who declined to provide troops and financial aid, Wallace vowed that "we're not only going to cut off every penny of foreign aid, but we're going to ask you to pay back that you've already gotten."

Wallace ranted against the federal government and "thousands of briefcase-toting bureaucrats who not only come to your state but to my state telling the average man on the street what he can do with his child, what he can do with his school, what he can do with his seniority and apprenticeship, business and labor unions . . . apportionment of his legislature . . . redistricting of his congressional district . . . and now they're going to tell you what you can do with your homes and your own property."

All roads to the White House led through Nebraska's rural expanse, and through the wards and precincts of its largest city, Omaha, population 340,000.

Wallace announced that he would be in Omaha on Monday, March 4. His prime-time rally, to petition to have his third party on the primary ballot, would take place downtown at the Civic Auditorium, a plain modern edifice that then was the city's largest convention center. The auditorium was two blocks east of Central High, a stroll down Capitol Avenue, close enough for students to catch the baby scent of new history.

The Civic Auditorium was to be the site of the state Class A basketball tournament, scheduled to start three days after Wallace's rally. If Central was to win its first hoops title since 1912, it would be where Wallace roused a crowd not apt to be fans of the Rhythm Boys.

The culture war, national politics, and high school basketball soon would converge at a building, in unexpected fashion. But in a symbolic sense, it already had, in a nickname.

"If they had called me a Rhythm Boy I wouldn't have liked it," recalled Dillard. "But 'Rhythm Boys' was cool."

6

Get on Board

To the victors went the spoils at Sadie's Home Bakery, the Biddle family business. A few mornings after the Prep game, Dillard, Frazier, and a couple of others stopped by Sadie's to pick up John Biddle, who arose early to help his mother, father, and siblings. Sadie Biddle laid out a pan of sweet buns—and not for the first time—that vanished in an instant.

"Hot and greasy," Dillard recalled. "She gave us so many I don't know how she stayed in business."

Sadie's buns nourished the Rhythm Boys, as did the neighborhood, the Near North Side, where they came of age. This was Omaha's inner city, a black oasis in the rural and white Midwest. Its de facto boundaries were Sixteenth Street on the east, Thirtieth Street on the west, Cuming Street on the south, and Ames Avenue on the north. Most of the city's thirty-four thousand black residents, and most of Central's black students, lived there, for better or worse.

Its main drag, North Twenty-fourth Street, was the bakery's address, and a way of life that, by 1968, was under siege.

"They called it the Deuce," Phil Griffin recalled. "A little bit of everything went on there. Someone might have a car and

John Biddle worked at his family bakery on North Twenty-fourth Street. Photo courtesy of Carlos Dillard.

you'd cruise from one end to another—see who you might run into."

"That's where you went on Friday night," recalled Curt Melton, Griffin's classmate. "You'd stand and drink and holler at women. It was a place to go for excitement and trouble."

Historically, the Near North Side was Omaha's Ellis Island. First came the Irish, Scandinavians, and Germans, in the 1870s and 1880s. Italians and Jews came at the onset of the twentieth century. African Americans migrated north in the years after World War I, lured by packinghouse and railroad jobs.

Each new group, in search of a better life, viewed North Twenty-fourth as a "street of dreams," the title of a 1994 documentary film by Nebraska Educational Television. To an extent, each had succeeded, but in 1968 the African American experience was a work in progress and a study in frustration. The Biddles exemplified both success and the struggle ahead.

In the early 1930s, Sadie Montgomery arrived in Omaha from Fort Worth, Texas, and Dave Biddle from Little Rock, Arkansas. After they married, Dave worked as a plumber and swim coach, while Sadie was a baker — one of just a few blacks — at Union Station, the Art Deco railroad terminal on South Tenth Street. They bought a two-story duplex at 2511 Charles Street, where John, the eighth of nine children, was born in 1950. Sadie and Dave put money down on a commercial building, the former site of a Dairy Queen, and opened the bakery in 1962.

The shop was closed on Mondays. Other days Sadie arose at 2:00 a.m. to bake cakes, donuts, rolls, buns, and brownies. She opened the door at 6:00 a.m., closed it at 5:00 p.m., and cooked her family's meals during business hours. Her husband and children helped but her ninety-hour week took its toll.

"I had to rub her feet," Biddle recalled.

As small business and commercial property owners, John Biddle's parents were a minority among a minority. Whites, many of them Jewish, who lived in the western and northern neighborhoods, still owned a number of businesses and most of the commercial buildings — a source of frustration.

"White owners wouldn't sell to blacks," Biddle recalled.

More typical were Biddle's uncle, and the fathers of Willie Frazier and the Moss brothers, who worked at packinghouses in south Omaha, as butchers. At a time when race was a barrier throughout the workplace, for thousands of black workers these were the best jobs available. Though the pay was modest, and the work strenuous, most adopted the attitude of Jessie

Franklin Gauff, who packaged hotdogs at Swift, and did not complain.

"Your people worked in the cotton fields—this is a step up," Jessie told her daughter Jawanda.

Darryl Eure visited his father, Al Eure, a butcher, at the packinghouse one afternoon.

"The cow came in on a chute," recalled Eure. "A guy with a sledgehammer would pop that cow in the head and lift it up and put it on a chain. Dad had on this bib apron and boots and his job was to cut the bull's jugular vein. The blood would come out—Dad would be standing in blood up to his chest—and then he had the job of cutting all around the bull's head to take it off."

At the end of his shift, Al Eure came home exhausted.

"His hands were hard like cement from holding those knives all day," Eure recalled. "When he came home he would take razor blades and cut the calluses off his hands and off the bottom of his feet, which he got from standing in those boots all day."

James Griffin, Phil's father, worked at a packinghouse upon his arrival from Arkansas in the mid-1950s. Later he found a job as a machine oiler at Western Electric, a maker of telephone products. James Griffin was one of a handful of blacks at Western Electric, one of Omaha's largest employers, and may have been the first at his specific job, according to his son.

Jobs were more plentiful at the Union Pacific Railroad, headquartered in Omaha since it partnered to build the first transcontinental rail line in the 1860s. The UP offered daily service to Chicago, San Francisco, Los Angeles, Portland, and

Denver. Each train required an engineer, brakeman, conductor, fireman, baggage man, cooks, waiters, chair-car porters, sleeping-car porters, and attendants. Most of the cooks, baggage men, waiters, porters, and attendants were black.

Dillard's girlfriend, Barbara Essex, was the daughter of a chair-car porter, Robert Essex, who worked the Portland line. Unionized since the 1920s, porters made relatively good wages.

One summer Barbara vacationed in California with her mother, Beverly, and returned to a surprise.

"My father had redone my whole bedroom with new furniture and yellow carpet," Essex recalled. "I thought we were rich—I knew we were."

William Graves, the father of Central student Bill Graves, came from Texas to work as a private car attendant. He took up golf at nearby Miller Park, and became one of the top black amateur golfers in Omaha. Al Eure, a friend of William Graves, marveled at the lifestyle of railroad workers.

"Those railroad guys come in and everybody got to stand back because they got the money," Al Eure would say with a chuckle. "They come to town and get all the girls."

Steady paychecks anchored the community in the 1950s and early 1960s. Central student Raymond Parks's grandfather and uncles worked as porters and cooks; one uncle, James Smith, was the personal chef of the Union Pacific president. Parks's father worked at the Wilson packinghouse for thirty years, a time when the Near North Side, to a boy, seemed safe and secure.

"It was almost like 'Leave it to Beaver on the North Side,'" recalled Parks. "We made go-carts, and we had sleds, and we fished in Carter Lake."

East of Sixteenth Street ran railroad tracks and not much else. Kids shot birds with BB guns, and hopped boxcars for a ride to the Storz Brewery.

An abandoned boxcar at Twenty-fourth and Burdette was converted into a restaurant. After it went out of business, Parks and his buddies broke in and claimed it as a clubhouse, but not for long.

"One day we went down there and the hobos and bums had taken it over," Parks recalled.

Neighbors kept an eye out for one another, recalled Calvin Brown, younger brother of former Central player, Ben Brown. Residents left open their front doors without worrying about theft. On the streets kids couldn't get into too much trouble.

"You couldn't do nothing wrong without somebody telling on you," Brown recalled. "There was always somebody on a porch being nosy."

An unspoken "mothers' network" kept youth in line, recalled Phyllis Mitchell.

"His mother better not call my mother and find out he was acting up," Mitchell said. "I couldn't smart off to Dwaine Dillard's mother or nobody else's. You had to show a certain level of respect—you didn't roll your eyes or jerk your neck."

Excluded from white social institutions, Omaha's black community had its own, including a gala in which it elected a King Borealis and Queen Aurora. Black women joined the National Federation of Afro-American Women, while men belonged to the Benevolent and Protective Order of Elks, Eastern Star, Brotherhood of Sleeping Car Porters, and Dining Car Waiters Union.

Along North Twenty-fourth were stores for clothing, hardware, and auto parts, ice cream shops, laundries, drugstores, restaurants, bars, barbershops, beauty salons, shoe repair and package liquor businesses, pool halls, funeral homes, and offices for doctors, dentists, and lawyers. Mildred Brown's weekly newspaper, the *Omaha Star*, which covered the black community, was headquartered there. St. Benedict's Church and Rectory was a presence. Nearby were the YMCA, Boys Club, and Colored Old Folks Home. At least fifteen Christian churches, fundamentalist and evangelical, were in close proximity.

The gem of North Twenty-fourth was the red-bricked Jewell Building, home of the Dreamland Ballroom, where jazz greats Count Basie, Duke Ellington, Dinah Washington, and Earl Hines, as well as native son Preston Love, performed. The Near North Side attracted top musicians because of Omaha's location on the Union Pacific main line. In the 1940s and 1950s Dreamland was filled with crowds of four hundred and more, and not only Dreamland.

"The street is full of pool halls and bars, and on Friday night or Saturday night, when the people who worked in the packinghouses got their checks, they went right down to Twenty-fourth Street and drank half of it up," Gale Sayers (Central High class of '61) wrote in his autobiography.

In 1967 and 1968, Sayers, one of Central's greatest athletes, was an All-Pro running back and return specialist with the Chicago Bears, on his way to Hall of Fame enshrinement. But his youth on the Near North Side was marked by bitter hardship.

His family had moved from Kansas to Omaha in 1951 and rented a unit in the Thirtieth Street projects. As his father scratched out a living as a car polisher, they moved nine times in eight years, "and always, it seemed, going from bad to worse." His parents sank into despair, drank, and fought. His father played poker and lost money that would have bought food and coal for the furnace.

For food, Sayers and his older brother, Roger, shot sparrows and catbirds with BB guns. They fried the birds, along with chicken feet, which cost fifty cents for a hundred.

As a senior, in 1960, Sayers set a city scoring record as Central went undefeated. For each touchdown, Sayers won a certificate from a local drive-in for a "Pookie Burger," a double-decker hamburger. In three games Sayers scored three touchdowns, and after each game he gobbled three Pookie Burgers.

"One reason I enjoyed scoring so many touchdowns was that it kept me from going hungry in what was a difficult year at home," Sayers wrote.

In October 1967 Bob Gibson was an All-Star right-hander who led the St. Louis Cardinals into the World Series and won three games en route to Hall of Fame election. Gibson, who grew up fatherless on the Near North Side, and graduated from Tech in 1955, wrote in his autobiography of a rat-infested house on Hamilton Street.

"We nailed tin cans over holes in the floors to keep the rats out, but they ate through the cans and one of them bit me in the ear while I was sleeping," Gibson wrote.

After the Cardinals won the World Series, Gibson was honored in front of the county courthouse downtown. Carrie Campbell, who grew up on Twenty-eighth Street, her father a custodian at the WOW building, and her mother an owner of a licensed day-care business, presented Gibson flowers.

Schooled at St. Benedict's and Mercy High, and later to become Frazier's wife, Campbell described a youth more comfortable than Gibson's, yet austere.

"To get a cake at a bakery was a big deal—at least to our family," Campbell recalled.

For Omaha youths like Sayers and Gibson, and countless others on the Near North Side, sports helped kids forget who had more or less. Near North Side grade schools, Kellom, Lothrop, Long, and Howard Kennedy, and junior highs, Horace Mann and Tech, offered four or five sports. Logan and Kountze parks were hotbeds of sandlot basketball and football, though the Kountze field, Sayers wrote, was pocked and full of cockleburs that stuck to clothes, arms, and legs. Kellom Park had the only swimming pool on the Near North Side.

North Side YMCA, where Bob Gibson's older brother Josh coached, and Gene Eppley Boys Club, a modern facility with a wider range of recreation, were popular.

In 1968, Near North Side athletes filled the rosters at three high schools, Central, Tech, and North, as well as the pages of the *Omaha Star*. The *Star*'s enthusiasm was such that it named its "first annual Sepia Prep All-Star team." Dillard, described as an "all-everything scoring machine" led the first team, joined by two Tech players, Ernie Britt and James Bonner, and one each from Boys Town and Thomas Jefferson of Council Bluffs. The second team included Frazier and Griffin, as well as Tech's Johnny Rodgers and Gerald Turner.

The All-Star team, and sports in general, helped buoy the Near North Side as hard times descended. After gains in the years after World War II, the neighborhood's toehold on the working class, never too secure, began to slip. Large meatpackers scaled down and moved out. Cudahy closed in 1967, and Armour was scheduled to close later in 1968. Swift's closure was a year away. About 6,500 jobs, many held by black workers, vanished from 1955 to 1969.

Al Eure lost his job at Cudahy but went to work for a small independent meatpacker, at a lesser wage. With the household budget pinched, Dorothy Eure, Darryl's mother, shopped at rummage sales. One day, as Darryl dressed after gym class, another boy tapped him on the shoulder.

"You're wearing my shirt," the boy said.

The other boy was certain because his nametag was on Eure's shirt. Eure tore off the nametag, but the story of the second-hand shirt circulated through Central's halls, and embarrassed him.

Those without packinghouse or railroad jobs made do, or didn't. James Hunter, Roy's father, worked two and three jobs at a time, as a custodian, to support his wife and four children. "Most of the time Dad was at work, which unfortunately meant we didn't spend a lot of time with him," Hunter recalled.

For the city as a whole, median income increased by almost 62 percent during the 1960s, from $6,300 to $10,200. But for the area around the Bryant Basketball Center, median income froze at $3,600.

A 1964 survey showed that if not for restrictive real estate covenants, 29 percent of Near North Side residents would move out, and that 48 percent wanted to move but did not have enough money. Another survey showed that nearly half of Omaha's deteriorated housing was on the Near North Side.

Dreamland Ballroom's closure in 1965 signaled a change in the North Twenty-fourth Street economy, as well as musical

Motown wannabes (*from left*) Jerry Moss, John Biddle, Ralph Hackney, Phil Griffin, and Dwaine Dillard. Photo courtesy of Carlos Dillard.

tastes. Early in 1966 Ernie Chambers likened the neighborhood to a powder keg, which could "blow up" if conditions did not improve.

Political impotence heightened black frustration. The forty-nine-member unicameral legislature had one black senator—Edward W. Danner—and the state board of education had one black member. Blacks held no seats on the Omaha City Council, Douglas County Board of Health and Board of Commissioners, Metropolitan Utilities District, Omaha Airport Authority, Sarpy County Board of Commissioners, Omaha Public Power District, and Omaha County Planning Board.

Central's starters lived on the Near North Side. *From left*: Coach Jim Martin, Coach Warren Marquiss, Phil Griffin, Dwaine Dillard, John Biddle, Roy Hunter, and Willie Frazier. Reprinted with permission of the *Omaha Central High School O-Book*.

By the spring of 1967, black unemployment and underemployment were estimated at 25 percent, while the city's overall rate was 2.6 percent.

After the 1966 riot, the city published a report that outlined blighted areas—defined as "below community standards of suitability for living or doing business." Blighted areas included the entire Near North Side, and no neighborhoods west of Forty-second Street.

Whites found it "uncomfortable" to visit the Near North Side, wrote Jack Todd in the *Daily Nebraskan*, the University of Nebraska's student newspaper.

"Walk down North Twenty-fourth street in Omaha, talk to housewives in project apartments, eat in Negro cafes," Todd wrote. "The urgency, hopelessness, and despair of the Negro boils through surface hostility. Men stripped of their pride by years of low-paying menial jobs or unemployment look at white intruders carefully, glare for a split second, and turn away."

It was in this malaise that the Rhythm Boys became a source of entertainment and escape. It had taken awhile — through much of the season Central's crowds had been 85 percent white. Now, as the season approached its climax, people were ready — the Near North Side got on board.

Since the neighborhood had flipped from white to black in the post–World War II years, only Tech had won a state basketball title, in 1963, and its starting five had included one white. Now Central was favored to win the title with an all-black starting five.

The percentage of black fans shot up as Central dispatched Benson, 79–64, and Burke, 55–31, at the end of the regular season. From the court, Biddle scanned the crowds and saw twice as many black faces as before.

"Our community finally turned out," Biddle recalled.

Two faces — Sadie and Dave Biddle's — weren't there, for a reason their son, a child of the Near North Side, understood.

"They had to work."

7

Jupiter Aligns

On the first Sunday morning in March, Dillard showed up at the home of a classmate, Jerry "Moose" Raznick, to celebrate and relax. Their friendship was as simple—and complicated—as the skin they exchanged, white palm on black.

It had been a good week, as Central coasted through the district play-offs. Dillard had thirty-two points and twenty-five rebounds, and Frazier seventeen points and thirteen rebounds, in a first round blowout of Omaha Bryan, 73–47. Next was the district final, a 66–43 victory over Omaha Benson, in which Dillard logged twenty-two points, eighteen rebounds, and six blocked shots before he fouled out with three minutes left. The *World-Herald* reported that Dillard was "blocking shots as if he were swatting flies."

Raznick lived in the predominantly Jewish neighborhood known as Bagel, or Bagel Hill, north of Underwood Avenue and Cass Street, and south of Western Avenue, between Fifty-seventh and Sixty-ninth streets. Developed in the 1950s, with one- and two-story ranch houses, large driveways, and spacious lawns, Bagel thrummed with ambition and pretense. Its wide streets were suited to teenagers who cruised in Detroit-made "muscle" cars, as well as to so-called street parties, in which dozens of teens parked at curbside, usually along Glenwood Avenue, and practiced the timeless art of hanging out. Vikki Dollis, who lived in an older neighborhood near Forty-fifth and Walnut, wrote of the lure of Bagel the prior August:

About 3 this afternoon Nancy and I were just sitting around Field Club and she got the bright idea to go tandem riding. So we left at 4 and headed for Bagel (where all the Jewish kids live). We thought it would be great using up all those calories and seeing everybody too. But just our luck, we got out there and got a flat tire. That was o.k. though because we took it over to Dave Katz's house and ended up staying there. Everyone was at his house and it was so much fun, I wish we lived out there.

The Raznick home, a three-bedroom ranch, reflected Bagel's affluence, and the success of Morris Raznick's business, Omaha Meat Packing, a small independent operation. When Dillard arrived, Morris knew the drill. He made a run to Rothman's Deli and returned with bagels, corned beef, pastrami, lox, and cream cheese. Those were the delicacies his son and Dillard savored, and on this Sunday, their appetites were large.

"My Dad unpacked the food and it was gone in a minute," Raznick recalled.

As Dillard ate he admired Raznick's home.

"This is nice."

"You'll do better," Raznick said.

"You think?"

"What's to stop you?"

"College."

"You'll have your pick," Raznick said.

"School and me don't get along."

Jerry Raznick hosted the Rhythm Boys at his Bagel neighborhood home. Reprinted with permission of the *Omaha Central
High School O-Book.*

"Won't matter."

Dillard looked hopeful.

"Win state," Raznick said. "You'll have your pick."

Dillard's friendship with Raznick, outgoing and gregarious,
a former football player and a member of a Jewish fraternity
called Rayim, was genuine. The Rhythm Boys were comfortable
in visits to Bagel, a journey across social barriers and attitudes
that seemed to change by the hour. They often could be found,
weather permitting, at the full-length asphalt outdoor court of
Gary Riekes (Westside High School class of '69), the son of a

wealthy manufacturer. On winter nights they gathered at one or another of the homes, in well-appointed family rooms, and relished state-of-the-art sound systems and color televisions, not to mention ample refrigerators.

One evening Dillard and Biddle were dinner guests at the Bagel home of Danny Rubin, whose father ran a lucrative business in discounted home goods. With Rubin's parents out of town, the housekeeper cooked for the three teenagers. Dillard and Biddle ate prime rib for the first time.

Afterward, in Rubin's bedroom, Dillard and Biddle admired his wardrobe of expensive sweaters, shirts, trousers, socks, and shoes. Biddle removed his shoes and socks to try on Rubin's. That's when Rubin noticed the scars and calluses on Biddle's feet.

"What happened to your feet?"

"Hand-me-downs," Biddle said.

It was not surprising that Central's Jewish students were basketball fans. The only two white players on varsity, Harvey Josin and Jeff Krum, both juniors, were Jewish. The two varsity student managers, Bob Jacobson and Mike Sherman , also were Jewish.

Jews and blacks shared a history as persecuted minorities, and more. Their histories in Omaha had tangible intersections: the Near North Side, where the Jews had lived until after World War II and where they still owned businesses and rental properties; and Central, where they had been classmates for most of the twentieth century. A third intersection was the meatpacking industry, in which several independent operations were owned by Jews, such as Morris Raznick, and employed blacks. Sherman's family owned another independent, Cornhusker Packing.

The Jewish community, which numbered around seven thousand and was close-knit, tended to support progressive housing and job legislation. One Jewish leader, Norman Hahn (Central class of '41), chairman of the Omaha Human Relations Board, publicly rebuked white legislators, city councilors, and realtors who opposed fair housing measures. Rabbi Sidney Brooks, head of the reform Temple Israel, was an outspoken advocate of integration in schools and neighborhoods. Virtually no Jews supported George C. Wallace.

Nick Rips (Central class of '38), who owned an optical factory on the southern edge of downtown, personified Jewish empathy toward blacks. "One day, early on, (he) looked out over his workers and decided there was still something missing: blacks. With that, he walked around the factory and to each supervisor gave a very specific instruction: hire blacks. The order was carried out and very quickly blacks and, shortly thereafter, Hispanics, mostly women, became a significant part of the workforce," wrote Mike Rips (Central class of '72), Nick's third son, in his ode of filial wonder, *The Face of a Naked Lady: An Omaha Family Mystery.*

Nick's second son, Harlan, did his bit to help Jewish-black relations when Dillard was seated across the aisle in a history class.

"We had a test and Dwaine asked if he could scope off mine," Rips recalled. "I said sure."

A few days later the tests were returned: Rips received the highest score, a one, and Dillard got a four, one above the lowest.

"What happened?" Rips asked.

"Your answers didn't look right, so I changed mine," Dillard said.

Jewish-black relations became strained after the 1966 riot, when Jewish shops on the Near North Side were firebombed. Jews were not sure if Jewish shops were targeted, or if they just were caught up in the mayhem. The result was that many of the remaining Jewish businesses, such as Adler's Bakery on North Twenty-fourth Street, moved out.

Black anger toward Jews was tied to substandard housing. Many Jewish-owned rentals on the Near North Side did not meet stiffened city codes. One Jewish landlord, Sonny Gerber, a car dealer whose daughter, Debbie, was a Central senior, would see an Ernie Chambers–led picket of his Fairacres home later in the spring.

Moreover, blacks pointed to Bagel, as well as other neighborhoods where Jews lived—Fairacres, Dundee, and Happy Hollow—as segregated. The real estate developer who had turned down Bob Boozer was a Jewish man, Milton Simon. While it was true that not a lot of black homebuyers could afford to buy a home in Bagel, those able perceived that they would not be welcome even if they found a seller.

"I would guess there were none or few black people who wanted to look at homes there," recalled Diana Hahn (Central class of '41), wife of Norman Hahn.

The Hahns had well-to-do black friends, such as Dr. Claude Organ Jr. and his wife Betty, Dr. Earle G. Person, Rodney Wead (Central class of '53), and Bob and Charlene Gibson. Charlene served on the Human Relations Board with Norm Hahn. On a few occasions the Hahns hosted their black and Jewish friends at their home in Bagel, until they realized their Jewish friends were uncomfortable.

"Our Jewish friends had a hard time mingling—they sat off by themselves," Diana Hahn recalled.

Over time, the Hahns felt ostracized in Bagel.

"I had the sense socially that we were estranged," Diana Hahn recalled. "Nobody told me directly, but you pick things up when people leave you out of parties you used to go to."

Black anger stung Omaha's Jewish leaders of the mid-1960s, according to Steve Riekes (Central class of '58), the cousin of Gary Riekes, and an attorney active in Jewish affairs.

"The old Jewish community could not understand this burning and rage and how to adjust to it, and young Jews were perplexed," said Riekes.

Black-Jewish relations were further complicated by an upheaval amongst Jews that did not involve blacks, but owed to the black movement. For decades Jewish leaders, in the face of anti-Semitism, had suppressed their Jewish identities and embraced assimilation. In the 1960s, Roger Lowenstein wrote in *Buffett*, his biography of Warren Buffett, "Omaha's Jews were neither entirely ready to assimilate nor entirely welcome in gentile society." Jews were not admitted to the Omaha and Happy Hollow country clubs, and in return, barred admission of gentiles to their own Highland Country Club.

Though Omaha had elected a Jewish mayor, John R. Rosenblatt, throughout the 1950s, a list of "Twenty Influentials"—the city's power elite—drawn up in 1966 by a local journalist, included just one Jew, Morris E. Jacobs, chairman of Bozell and Jacobs Advertising.

The arriviste status of Jews fed an insecurity that was evident to Raymond Parks, who grew up around Jewish shopkeepers on North Twenty-fourth, uncertain of their race.

"When I talked to people I wanted to piss off I would say I went to school with white folks and Jews," Parks recalled.

While the old guard clung to assimilation, a group of young Turks, led by Nick Newman, the head of a supermarket chain, wanted it both ways. They wanted in to the gentile private clubs, and at the same time they wished to cast off assimilation and embrace their heritage, openly and with pride. Among their priorities was establishment of a Jewish day school.

The turning point came in June 1967 when Israel scored a stunning and decisive military victory over its Arab neighbors in the Six-Day War. The victory not only assured the immediate survival of Israel, it galvanized a new era of pride among American Jews and made it easier for young leaders such as Newman to move ahead. Soon, young Jews organized a march to Memorial Park, with Israeli flags and banners aloft, that would have been unthinkable before. Within a couple of years, a Jewish day school would be opened, and the Highland Country Club would admit a gentile, Buffett, a native Omahan and legend-to-be investor, whose circle of Jewish friends included Newman. Buffett's admission, at his request, enabled him to compel the gentile private clubs to open membership to Jews.

"The Jewish community learned something from the blacks," Riekes recalled. "That it is all right to be who you are and to be proud of who you are and to be public with who you are."

By 1968 Jewish and black leaders were on their own cultural and political trajectories. Nonetheless, Jewish and black students at Central reached out tentatively, and curiously, to one another. The basketball team provided a common ground, as prior teams had at Central. The difference was this team's frequent presence in Bagel.

As a sixteen-year-old junior at Central, and a Jewish resident of Bagel, I was passionate about the team. The most obvious reason was that team members Jeff Krum and Harvey Josin were friends.

Krum's mother, Adelaide, and my late mother, Mildred, had met in a maternity ward in Steubenville, Ohio, in May 1948, as they awaited the birth of their first children. Denny Marantz and Debbie Krum were born days apart. In April 1951 Jeff Krum arrived at Ohio Valley General Hospital, and I was born in August 1951. The young families were close, until the Krums moved from Ohio to Des Moines in 1954, and Stan Krum took an executive position with Younkers, a Midwest department store chain headed by his wife's brother. In 1961 the Krums moved to Omaha, where Stan took charge of Kilpatrick's, part of the Younkers chain.

In March 1963 my mother succumbed to breast cancer. My father, Robert Marantz, closed our family department store and moved his three children to Omaha, at the invitation of Stan and Adelaide Krum. He went to work at Kilpatrick's, while Denny enrolled at Central and resumed his friendship with Debbie, and I enrolled at Lewis and Clark Junior High and built a friendship with Jeff. My sister, Mindy, attended Dundee Elementary.

In the spring of 1964 my father met the widow Harriet Katz. Her husband, Louis Katz, had died in a car accident in 1963, leaving her with three children, Susan, Marilyn, and David B.

Attracted by a shared sense of loss, and by their needs as single parents, my father and Harriet courted, and married in September 1964. The four of us moved into Harriet's five-bedroom ranch on Sunset Trail, in the middle of Bagel. Thus did my father connect himself, and his children, to a sturdy trunk of Omaha history.

Harriet was born in Omaha in 1924, the first child of Aaron and Lena Shafer. Seventeen-year-old Aaron Shafer had emigrated from Russia in 1913 to avoid conscription in the czar's army, and had worked as a tailor. To earn citizenship, he enlisted in the U.S. Army in 1917. Near the end of World War I he was gassed at Meuse-Argonne and suffered a permanent disability, which paid him a monthly government check the rest of his life, though he was able to run various businesses. In 1921 he married Lena Krasne, the daughter of an immigrant shoemaker from Aurora, Illinois.

Aaron and Lena raised their two daughters, Harriet and Geraldine (Gerry), born in 1926, in a white, two-story, wood-frame house at 2761 Webster Street, in the heart of the Near North Side. The street was all white and half Jewish, but black families lived nearby, and both Shafer girls had black friends at the integrated Webster Street Elementary School. The two sisters were raised as Orthodox Jews and attended services at three different synagogues.

On Saturdays Lena took her daughters downtown, bought them five-cent tickets to the Orpheum Theater, handed them a salami sandwich and a nickel's worth of candy, and went off to shop, usually at Brandeis Department Store. The girls sat through two shows before their mother picked them up.

On Sundays Aaron piled his two daughters into his Chevrolet and drove them to a deli on Twenty-fourth Street, where they bought pickles, rye bread, pickled herring, lox, and cream cheese. As a child Gerry noticed that blacks shopped on Twenty-fourth Street, but rarely ventured in to the deli.

Harriet entered Central in the fall of 1938 and Gerry followed a year later. Among Gerry's classmates was Sylvia "Babe" Blumkin, youngest daughter of Rose Blumkin, better known as "Mrs. B," who had just started a business that would blossom into the iconic Nebraska Furniture Mart.

"They had a big house at Thirty-third and something, with a huge furnished basement," Gerry recalled. "We used to go there and dance. Mrs. B's husband (Isadore) was a real sweetie. He provided all the refreshments."

During high school Harriet worked as a salesperson at a downtown women's clothing store. After she graduated from Central in 1942 she enrolled at nearby Creighton University but, without financial support from the penurious Aaron, dropped out in her first semester. She took a job as a secretary at an insurance agency, waited for World War II to end, and prayed for the safe return of her high school beau, Louis Katz, who was stationed in Europe. Katz, born and raised in Omaha, came back early in 1946. In March 1946 he and Harriet were married.

Soon Lou Katz ventured into the war-surplus business, with a start-up loan from his brother-in-law, Alan Zalkin. He and his partner, Sam Goodman, established four Ranks stores in Omaha and eastern Iowa that became profitable. Lou and Harriet moved from a rented apartment and bought a stylish, brick, two-story colonial on Country Club Avenue, near Benson, in what eventually became a national historic district.

Their journey toward affluence and away from the Near North Side was mirrored by hundreds of Jewish couples in the postwar years. But not all Jews in Omaha were in a position to ride the boom to prosperity. Some were occupied with day-to-day survival.

Ben and Emma Josin were good at survival—very good. Both were Holocaust survivors determined to get beyond their nightmarish past. Ben, who was born in Poland in 1919, lost his mother, brother, and two sisters in Nazi work camps. Emma, born in Lithuania in 1924, lost three brothers—one who was killed in the underground resistance. Both spent six years in work camps, where they met, and were spared because they were strong workers. When Ben was laid low by typhoid, a sympathetic German guard brought him soup and sheltered him in a hole under his bunk.

After the war, Ben and Emma were quartered in a home for refugees in Bamberg, Germany, where they married. They were given a choice for resettlement between Israel and America, and though Emma leaned toward Israel, Ben believed America offered a better chance to get ahead.

"Too many Jews in Israel—I need goyim to make a living," Ben told Emma.

Sponsored by the Omaha Jewish Community Center, Sherman Poska, and Dr. Abraham Greenberg, the young couple arrived in Omaha in 1949.

"We're in the Wild West—the frontier," Emma told Ben.

Ben found a job as an upholsterer at American Upholstery, a furniture manufacturing plant, while Emma worked as a seamstress and made mattress covers at Serta Mattress. They rented a house on Twenty-eighth Street, in the Near North Side, and saved their money. Ben turned the garage into an upholstery shop, and after he worked a full day at the plant, he ran his own small business out of the garage in the evenings. Between four miscarriages, Emma gave birth to Harvey in 1951 and Sherry in 1954.

By the mid-1950s Ben's garage business enabled him to quit his job at the factory, which angered his employers, who predicted that the immigrant with the sixth-grade education and heavy accent would fail on his own. Ben bought a home with a storefront at Forty-sixth and Cuming, at the eastern edge of the Dundee neighborhood, and set up business. His timing was good. Affluent Jewish couples, such as Harriet and Lou Katz, moved into the new subdivision of Bagel in the mid 1950s. Their plush homes required new furniture, or makeovers of old furniture. Within a couple of years Ben had three employees and a toehold on the upper middle class.

Ben's success enabled his son, Harvey, to indulge in something absent from his own youth—organized sports. Tall, sturdy, and possessed of a gregarious, excitable personality, Harvey excelled in basketball. He played on a team at Lewis and Clark Junior High whose star center, Krum, was coveted by several high school coaches. Krum, tall, fast, and athletic, led his ninth-grade team to the 1966 city championship, as did Bruce Muskin, while Josin and Steve Nogg played a backup role, and I came off the end of the bench. The team included another backup, Don Marquiss (Benson class of '69), whose father, the head coach at Central, watched from the bleachers.

With Krum ticketed for Central, Warren Marquiss said a silent "thank-you" and penciled him in to his future lineup.

As Harvey's basketball game developed, his father Ben's business game got bolder. In the mid-1960s he moved his family to a larger and more modern house, close to Bagel, and pondered a new business. Instead of upholstering furniture, he wanted to wholesale fabric to upholsterers and furniture makers, which would be less labor intensive and more profitable. But before he made the leap he consulted with his son. Ben knew that if his plan worked out he would need help growing the business.

"Are you with me?" he asked his son.

"I'll go with you out of college," Harvey promised.

As Ben expected, wholesale fabric supply was more profitable, and he acquired security enough to make him almost forget how tenuous his life had been. Less expected was the progress of his son's basketball career. Harvey developed a grooved and accurate jumper from fifteen to twenty feet, took an occasional sniff at defense, and was a surprise addition to the Central varsity in the fall of 1967. But basketball was foreign to Ben and he found it hard to fathom. Harvey pointed out his name in the newspaper box score and Ben shook his head.

"No, you're not playing with those 'schwartzes'—I don't believe it," Ben would say.

By the middle of the season Ben began to understand that his son was a "godl" at Central. He decided to attend his first game—the Central-Prep showdown of the state's number one and number two ranked teams. But when he got to Norris Junior High the stands already were filled. Though he informed the ushers that his son played on the team, they guided him toward the auditorium for the closed-circuit telecast. His first glimpse of his son in a Central uniform was on a screen.

The harrowing and heroic past of Josin's parents was not known in any detail to his friends, such as myself, and certainly not to his teammates, such as Dillard. But most black students understood that Jews had gone through something similar to the black experience of oppression.

"I mingled with Caucasians and Jews, but it was the Jewish kids who especially accepted us," Dillard recalled. "I think it was because Jewish people went through the same things we went through."

I was typical of most Jewish students in that my first contact with black peers was at Central. I had lived in all-white neighborhoods and attended all-white schools. The only black person I knew as a child was our housekeeper, Blanche, who was like a mother to me, until one day she vanished, off our budget, my heart broken.

Guidance was thin at home. I am sure my father and stepmother considered themselves tolerant on matters of race. They were enthusiastic and polite—overly so—when my older brother, Denny, brought a black student, John Orduna, home for dinner. But they chose not to be involved in progressive politics or causes and had no black friends or acquaintances. They advised us to exercise caution, and even lock our doors, when we drove through the Near North Side.

When I started at Central, in the fall of 1966, I was nervous and curious about black students, but I don't recall that they were a source of angst, as were grades, girls, clothes, cars, and popularity. Like all teenagers, I wanted to fit in, but without a discernable talent—in athletics, music, theater, or in most academics—it was a puzzle. A member of my Jewish fraternity, Gary Soiref, recruited me as a manager of the junior varsity basketball team. As I handed out towels, gathered uniforms, socks, and jockstraps, pumped air into basketballs, and charted shots and rebounds, I came to know the black basketball players. Sometimes I would ride with another manager, Bob Jacobson, as he picked them up or dropped them off at their homes. This gave me my first close-up look at the black neighborhoods, and what I saw were people and families, not statistics or lurid news reports.

As a junior I quit as basketball manager so that I could deliver ice cream to my father's vending machines after school. In social matters I was alone and adrift, except at basketball games. Inside the gym—and ballparks and stadiums—were energy, heat, light, youth, and optimism. Outside was everything else, which explained why, when it came time in journalism class to specialize, I chose sports. It joined my enthusiasm to a hopeful aptitude as a writer and gave me an identity. It pleased me that journalism was social—now I had a reason and method to be among people.

Race and politics were part of the world outside the gym, or so it seemed. I did not yet know that sports, race, and politics were entwined—from the ancient Olympics to Jack Johnson to Jesse Owens to Jackie Robinson—though Muhammad Ali had made me ponder the tenuous balance of individual rights and public obligation. At sixteen, there was much I did not know, or vaguely comprehended, about race and politics. I did not know, for instance, that the presence of the Rhythm Boys in Bagel was what Harry Edwards envisioned in the Revolt of the

George C. Wallace arrived at Eppley Airfield to the tune of "Dixie."
Reprinted with permission of the *Omaha World-Herald*.

Black Athlete. By virtue of their celebrity status, black athletes could create harmony and understanding beyond sports.

When Dillard visited Raznick on the first Sunday of March 1968, their friendship—and Jewish support of the Rhythm Boys—was on the cusp of Aquarius, a new age. But they were like me, teenagers not prone to deep thoughts, and more interested in the sports section spread out on Raznick's kitchen table.

Dillard, with a 22.9 conference scoring average, was named to the *World-Herald* All-Metro team by a unanimous vote of the coaches, along with Mike Peterson of Creighton Prep, Ernie Britt of Tech, George Jones of Benson, and Bob Anderson of Abraham Lincoln of Council Bluffs. Frazier received one vote.

Of Dillard, the newspaper reported: "The league's rebound king, the 6-7 Eagle also has been the heart of the Central barricade with a spectacular flair for blocking shots."

That afternoon, as Dillard and Raznick relaxed and watched the NBA Game of the Week, George C. Wallace flew in to Omaha.

When Wallace arrived at Eppley Airfield, to the tune of "Dixie," he was greeted by about a thousand supporters, as well as one hundred fifty protesters, black and white. The *Omaha Star* reported that "Negro youths led a group of students in a vocal version of 'We Shall Overcome' after the strains of 'Dixie' had blown south in the northerly breeze." Wallace fielded questions, labeled news reporters as "pseudo-intellectuals," and predicted that his support would come from Omaha's cab drivers, barbers, beauty operators, cops, firemen, farmers, and steelworkers.

Heading the security detail assigned to Wallace was Deputy Chief Monroe Coleman, one of about twenty-five blacks on the Omaha police force, and the father of Central High junior, Monroe Coleman Jr. Coleman was the department's first black deputy chief and had been the first black lieutenant to work the homicide unit.

After the airport press conference ended, Wallace slid into the back seat of a car. Coleman slid in next to him.

"Am I safe in this city?" Wallace asked.

"You're safe. My job is to see to that."

The irony of the nation's foremost segregationist seeking reassurance from a black police officer was not lost on Coleman. Years later he told a reporter, "I wanted to know what he was thinking."

8

"A Mongrel Unit"

The "Wallace for President" signs in the front yard of William and Mildred Glyn, just off Forty-fifth and Leavenworth, were "shameful" to their daughter, Sue, a senior at Central. But William Glyn was drawn to Wallace's segregationist views and welcomed his visit to Omaha.

William Glyn was a union ticket taker for Braniff Airways who had survived a rough upbringing. Born in Kansas, his mother had run off with another man when he was young, moved to California, and remarried. He and his stepfather did not get along, and at age twelve he was sent to live at Boys Town, the home for orphaned and indigent boys west of Omaha. He graduated from Boys Town High, enlisted in the infantry, and won a Purple Heart at the Battle of the Bulge. After the war he took classes at Creighton University and met Mildred Dusing, who had grown up on a farm in Iowa, come to Omaha as a government-sponsored nursing cadet, and become a nurse.

They married in the Catholic Church and had six children, the second of whom, Sue, a free spirit, was in love with Willie Frazier, and pregnant. But they didn't know of her pregnancy—yet. William and Mildred Glyn only knew that Sue had been dating the black son of a Near North Side mother who received welfare while William supported George C. Wallace for president.

"I forbid you to see this colored boy," the father said.

"But it was you who taught me that there was no difference between blacks and whites," she protested.

"Society won't tolerate it—you'll get hurt," the mother said.

Glyn was haunted by what she deemed to be her parents' "hypocrisy and prejudice"—their truth she found to be lies. And though her thoughts were preoccupied with her early-stage pregnancy, she was appalled at her father's support of Wallace. His candidacy was an affront, almost as if a hooded Klansman had declared for the presidency.

Wallace attracted voters such as William Glyn with a vow to keep whites and blacks apart. In his Alabama inaugural address, in January 1963, Wallace had said:

This nation was never meant to be a unit of one, but a unit of the many . . . and so it was meant in our racial lives. Each race, within its own framework, has the freedom to teach, to instruct, to develop, to ask for and receive deserved help from others of separate racial stations . . . but if we amalgamate into one unit as advocated by the communist philosophers, then the enrichment of our lives, the freedom for our development is gone forever. We become, therefore, a mongrel unit of one under a single all powerful government, and we stand for everything, and for nothing.

As the leering face of racism, Wallace was rebuked in Martin Luther King Jr.'s March on Washington speech on August 28, 1963. King said: "I have a dream that one day, down in Alabama, with its vicious racists, with its governor having his lips drip-

Sue Glyn was forbidden to date Willie Frazier by her father, a George Wallace supporter. Reprinted with permission of the *Omaha Central High School O-Book*.

ping with the words of 'interposition' and 'nullification,' one day right there in Alabama little black boys and black girls will be able to join hands with little white boys and white girls as sisters and brothers."

King's words resonated with African Americans who grew up in the Near North Side in the 1950s and 1960s—a time when they struggled with Omaha's own brand of racism and segregation. Until it was repealed in 1963, a Nebraska anti-miscegenation law prohibited whites from marrying blacks and Asians. It had been on the books since 1855, four years before the future Central High opened its doors.

Frazier appeared to have taken at least some of King's message to heart. He not only was the father of Glyn's unborn child, he was involved with another white girl, Dollis. Biracial dating was exciting and exotic. It also was scary, and Frazier proceeded with caution.

He and Glyn hung out at the homes of Frazier's friends, but not in public. Frazier refused.

"In terms of going to a movie or walking down the street—he wouldn't," Glyn recalled.

Once, at a football game, Glyn forgot herself and approached Frazier—the starting quarterback—on the sideline.

"He was livid that I would talk to him in front of the world," Glyn recalled. "He had a very healthy fear of white reaction to racially mixed couples."

Meanwhile, her sisters and white friends ostracized her, and at school she felt isolated. One day she found herself tumbling down one of Central's deep stairwells—propelled by a "surprise attack from behind."

"It was a black gay guy who may have resented my relationship with Willie," Glyn recalled, "or was put up to it by some black girls who were jealous."

The stigma—and appeal—of "miscegenation" was rooted deep in the psyches of blacks and whites. In his early teens Ken Secret visited the home of the daughter of one of the last white couples to live on the Near North Side. After Secret was driven home, he told his mother about his visit. Louise Secret was livid.

"You never do that again," she told him. "One line you never cross is white women. Eventually you get in trouble and society won't forgive you."

Louise came to Omaha from Arkansas as a thirteen-year-old, in 1935, in a Model T Ford that pulled a wagon and was filled with siblings, aunts, and uncles. When they reached Omaha, a sheriff invoked a local ordinance, arrested Louise's father, David Watson, and told the rest to turn around and leave by sundown. Fortunately, they saw an advertisement for Ralph Adams, Omaha's first black attorney. The family hired Adams, who went before a judge and secured Watson's release and the family's right to stay.

"What my mother told me was for my own good," Secret recalled. "She wasn't racist."

Ray Parks, a classmate of Secret and Frankie Weiner, recalled an episode from first grade, in the mid-1950s. Most of his classmates were black, but there was one blonde girl. After school, Parks told a black friend that he liked the little girl with blonde hair.

"You can't like her," the boy replied.

"Why?"

"Because she's white."

Parks ran home and asked his mother, Erline, if that was so. She nodded in the affirmative. Erline Parks's parents had come to Omaha from Alabama after World War I and had embraced caution in racial matters. Erline married Raymond H. Parks, a packinghouse worker, and they settled in the heart of the Near North Side at Twenty-fifth and Patrick. But in 1961 they moved into a white neighborhood at Sixteenth and Pinckney. They were the first black family on the street.

"It was rough for me," Parks recalled.

His problem resolved soon enough—within a year all the white families had moved out.

In 1919, the year Erline Parks's parents arrived from the Deep South, Lindbergh White's grandfather was caught up in the most violent racial incident Omaha has known. Richard Matlock, part Choctaw Indian, African American, and white, once had sparred with the black heavyweight champion Jack Johnson, whose dalliances with white women enraged white America before World War I. Matlock moved from Illinois to Omaha and met his wife, Matie, who had fled her family in Kansas because of an accident of birth—her parents and siblings had light skin and hers was dark.

One of Matlock's friends was an itinerant black packinghouse worker, Will Brown. In September 1919, at the end of a summer of white race riots across the country, a nineteen-year-old white woman claimed Brown mugged her male companion and raped her. Her allegation of black-on-white rape fueled sensational newspaper coverage, and inflamed local bigots. When police undertook to find Brown they sought out Matlock, who fled, but was cornered in a barn. Asked for Brown's whereabouts, Matlock clammed up, and was beaten.

"They beat him bad—he was broken in pieces," White recalled.

For the rest of his life Matlock was unable to do physical work as a result of the beating, White said, but he prided himself on his refusal to help authorities.

As events unfolded, Brown was captured and jailed at the Douglas County Courthouse downtown. It mattered not that Brown had severe rheumatism, moved with great effort, and seemed to have neither the dexterity nor energy to have committed the crime. A drunken mob of whites, estimated at several thousand, attacked the building, set it on fire, and forced police to hand over Brown. The mob hung Brown from a lamppost, shot him, set him on fire, and dragged his corpse through the streets. Mayor Edward P. Smith, who tried to intervene, was nearly lynched as well. Only the intervention of U.S. Army troops, who imposed martial law, prevented further violence against blacks.

The taboo of biracial sex, which fueled the murder of Will Brown, carried forward to the 1960s. When Delmar Givehand started to date Diane Jacobson, a Jewish girl from Bagel, in the autumn of 1967, he caught flak from both blacks and whites.

"There were people who resented it," Givehand recalled. "They were blatant about it. People would flat out say, 'I don't think it's right.'

"You heard it more from black people, but you sensed it more from white people. White people didn't want to approach you about it and give you an open opinion. But a number of black people felt they had to make statements about it."

One white person who openly opposed the relationship—and made it clear to Givehand—was Jacobson's father.

"He didn't think I would give Diane the best chance in life," Givehand recalled.

Among Givehand's black friends the most steadfast against biracial dating was Darryl Eure.

"We used to get on Delmar—he was chasing white girls," Eure recalled. "Back then you didn't do that. It was 'black power' and 'black is beautiful.'"

Eure was the son of a prominent civil rights activist, Dorothy Eure, one of the organizers of the Citizens Coordinating Committee for Civil Liberties, or 4CL. When Eure was twelve, he tagged along with his mother to city hall, where activists picketed city council chambers, singing "We Shall Overcome," in support of an open housing ordinance. Later, he was with her when about two thousand activists converged on the Douglas County Courthouse and demanded housing and jobs legislation. Their specific goals were delayed until national legislation was passed in 1964 and 1968, but their immediate impact was to energize the black community, awaken the white community to black needs, and focus the media on their issues.

In junior high, Eure read King's speeches and devoured writings by and about Mahatma Gandhi and Malcolm X, a native of Omaha. He met Ernie Chambers and became entranced with his militant rhetoric. When Eure started at Central in 1966 he found himself uncomfortable in the sea of white students.

"So I hung around blacks — it was more comfortable," Eure recalled.

However, Eure couldn't help but notice Carol Ramsey, a classmate who wore her blonde hair long down her back, was interested in the same social issues, and hung around his black friends. Ramsey was one of the twin daughters of parents active in progressive politics, William C. Ramsey (Central class of '30), an attorney, and Mary Jane Koperud Ramsey (Central class of '38). William Ramsey had been president of the Omaha Urban League in the early 1960s when the city hosted the organization's national convention.

Eure thought Ramsey was cute and funny, and before long he let down his guard and became friends with her. He got to know her so well, he recalled, that he easily could tell her apart from her fraternal twin, Julie.

One weekend Ramsey invited Eure to her plush home in the Fairacres subdivision, on the edge of Bagel, for a party. Eure could barely believe his eyes.

"Man, it was like, 'Look at this,'" Eure recalled.

After school one day Ramsey grabbed Eure's hand and pulled him in the direction of downtown.

"C'mon," she said. "We're going to be girlfriend and boy-friend."

Eure was startled, until he realized what Ramsey was up to. She wanted to walk hand-in-hand with Eure, through downtown, to make a political statement. She wanted to challenge the biases of anyone who chose to stare.

"So we walked down there, and man, did people stare," Eure recalled.

Their friendship was deep, and verged on flirtation, but it never crossed the line into a romance. For that Eure blamed himself.

"My mind couldn't get around a boyfriend-girlfriend thing—that's how stupid I was," Eure recalled.

In truth, Eure had been conditioned to avoid a romance, by history and common sense. Black males were caught in a bind—damned if they did and damned if they didn't. Black females were in less of a bind, if only because white males were more cautious or inhibited.

"There were a number of white guys who wanted to date black girls but couldn't work up the nerve," Givehand recalled. "They may have sensed that black girls were afraid to do it—more afraid than black guys."

Historically, whites and blacks had been cordial at school but had inhabited separate social spheres. That began to change in the mid 1960s, as signaled by the election of a black student, William Dodd, as king in Central's first homecoming, in 1963. The next year another black homecoming king, Carl Goodman, was elected. Goodman's queen, Mary Campbell, a white cheer-leader, suspected that the *World-Herald* omitted their photos, as was customary, because they were biracial.

In the spring of 1965 a white cheerleader, Kathleen Downs, became friendly with a black track star, Bobby Allen. Downs and a few white girlfriends began to visit the Near North Side homes of Allen, Chuck Alston, and Joe Orduna, all standout athletes. The teenagers played music and danced, and the black young men referred to themselves as the "Master Charmer's Yacht Club."

Allen and Downs drew close. After a track meet they met under a bleachers and he kissed her.

Later, he told Orduna, "I kissed Kathy."

"That's impossible," Orduna said. "White girls don't have any lips."

Allen and Downs began to date. He wrote her love poems and notes in class, but they were discreet about when and where they met. She wanted their relationship secret because she knew her father, a boiler-room worker at Veterans Hospital, would disapprove. The secret did not keep, as high school secrets tend not to, and soon both were summoned to the office of Bob Davis, an assistant principal.

"I have heard you two are seeing each other," Davis said.

They nodded.

"This cannot go on."

The two young people protested, angry and indignant. Davis waited until they fell silent, put his hand to a phone and looked at Downs.

"If you don't break up I'm going to call your parents," he said.

Downs, fearful of her father, backed down. With sad eyes, she turned to Allen, and said, "I'm sorry."

In the fall of 1967 a biracial group of males and females gathered on a regular basis near the stairwell outside the auditorium. A few of the white females began to socialize with black males outside of school, at which point the front office took action. Several of the white females were called in to explain their participation in a so-called zebra club.

"We were called to the office one person at a time," recalled Bonnie Knight. "It was more of a threat to not be involved than it was a questioning if it was happening."

Knight paid the warning no heed. Though she did not date the black young men in the group, she cultivated them as friends, particularly Marlyn Jackson and Vince Orduna, both standout athletes. They accompanied her after school as she walked to her father's office downtown, and occasionally were joined by another senior athlete, Dillard, who was, in Knight's recollection, "shy." Dillard, in fact, had a clandestine relationship with a Jewish girl, Jane Rice.

Dollis and Frazier, whose relationship deepened as 1968 began, ran into opposition from her parents, who lived in an all-white gentile neighborhood close to the Glyns. Dollis tried to keep her crush on Frazier a secret from her parents, who befriended biracial couples, but forbade her to date blacks. But when she invited Frazier to their house, they figured it out, as she wrote:

Sunday, January 21. It's unbelievable how my subconscious prepares me for everything. Now all my moods have significance and what I was unhappy about has happened. Tonite I asked my

parents if Willie and Dwaine and Janie could come over Thursday
night. Then hell broke loose! My mother got completely neurotic
and my father had a heart to heart talk with me about Willie.
When Willie called I just sat and cried because my dad told me
I had to end everything with him before my mom had a nervous
breakdown. But all I could tell Willie was that I had a fight with
my parents. Then my dad talked to me again and said that if
Willie would come over Thursday night he would explain the
situation to him. Then at least Willie will understand.

Dollis accused her parents of hypocrisy—of failing to practice the tolerance they preached. When her pastor at First United
Methodist Church supported her parents, she accused him of
hypocrisy as well.

"How can you preach racial tolerance?" Dollis asked him.

Dollis began to sense that her attraction to Frazier was linked
to her own troubled identity. Adopted at birth, Dollis grew
up feeling "different" from her two brothers, who were not
adopted. She had a tense relationship with her mother, who
worked in early childhood development, and who drove her
to excel. Dollis also suffered from depression, a genetic trait
handed down from biological parents she did not yet know,
and a condition that in those days often was undiagnosed, or
mistreated.

"Was it because I was adopted and felt out of place in my
own family that I was drawn to the world where blacks had
to stick together and be a 'brotherhood' in order to survive
the constant challenges to their right to be who they were?"
Dollis recalled. "Or was it my predisposition to depression
that sensitized me to the pain I sensed all of my black friends
suffering around me?

Vikki Dollis dated Willie Frazier against her parents' wishes. Reprinted with permission of the *Omaha Central High School O-Book*.

"Was it having a mother who communicated the message that I was never good enough that made me relate to how blacks at the time could never be as good as whites?

"There are lots of plausible reasons to explain why I chose to befriend blacks and love someone of a different color than me. They made me be open and willing to love Willie in spite of the incredible sacrifices I knew I'd have to make to be with him."

Frazier and Dollis continued to date, regardless of her parents. She liked how he was polite and respectful toward her and passed her affectionate and funny notes in the hallways.

"It shocked me how kind he was," Dollis recalled. "He never got mad."

Even more surprising was Frazier's sexual reticence. She had expected him to be sexually aggressive, because, stereotypically, black guys were supposed to be, and because she knew of his relationship with Glyn.

"That was the funniest thing about Willie—it was almost like he was afraid of me," Dollis recalled. "All we did was kiss—he was so in awe of me. I appreciated that."

Dollis' diary entry on March 3—the day Wallace flew in—described their sexual innocence:

Today was a beautiful day for me and Willie. After lunch I went and picked him up and we went to Carter Lake to play. It was warm and sunny and so first we ran around and then we just sat by the lake and talked. I wish we could spend all of our time together like that. Just being with him makes me happy, but we have fun playing. We went back to his house for a while but I had to go home so he kissed me good-bye. He kisses so good it makes me dizzy! There are many moments of doubt when I don't know if I'm right or wrong by loving him, but I know I can't stop so that should decide the answer. Besides I don't want to stop.

The opposite occurred, during the same period, when she went out with a white teen, Dollis recalled. This date mauled her, and she used her athleticism to fend him off, to his annoyance.

"Everybody knows you're giving it up to Willie," he said. "Why don't you give it up to a white guy?"

"No."

The biracial sexual taboo had a ripple effect—it justified and reinforced the elaborate boundaries that separated the races.

If the races could be kept apart, the taboo was less likely to be challenged. From that flowed the restrictive real estate covenants and bank redlining that kept blacks pinned in the inner city. Those practices, which mirrored Southern Jim Crow laws, had their roots in the 1920s, and long tenacious tentacles—long enough to thwart a black person as successful as Bob Boozer. A 1965 survey showed that Omaha had the same level of residential segregation as Birmingham, Alabama.

After Boozer was rebuffed in his effort to buy in a white Omaha neighborhood, a *Lincoln Journal Star* editorial concluded:

It is a lead-pipe cinch that if it is happening to Boozer, it is happening unnoticed to other Negroes whose names are not big sports news. Somehow it should take a little of the pride of Nebraskans out of their state as they wildly cheer the Cornhusker football team. Those Negro boys who are so great on Saturday afternoon are second-rate citizens when they want to live like other Nebraskans.

Sure enough, in February 1968, Sharon Rose, the black fiancée of Dick Davis, a star black running back for the University of Nebraska–Lincoln, was rejected in her application to rent a vacant apartment in south Omaha. Head coach Bob Devaney leaned on the owners in her behalf, to no avail. In the rejection, the owners cited "the nature of the ownership and the agreements among the owner and the insurance company which holds the mortgage, and the people who now lease in the building."

On Friday, February 16, as Central and Prep prepared for their showdown, sports columnist Wally Provost wrote: "Dick Davis and Miss Rose share a sinking sensation. The elevator taking them up in the world has started to shake and slip. Ambition . . . education . . . decency. How limited will be the rewards? How many opportunities will have a color restriction?"

The boundary extended from real estate to jobs. Even as union jobs at the packinghouses dried up, white-collar jobs remained scarce. If blacks could be denied white-collar jobs with decent wages and benefits, as found in the city's flourishing insurance industry, social contact would be minimized, and the issue of real estate in white neighborhoods would be moot—they couldn't afford it. Jawanda Gauff recalled that her aunt, with a degree to teach elementary school, failed to land a full-time job with Omaha Public Schools. At the start of the 1963–64 school year, only seventy-six black teachers were employed by the district, less than 5 percent of the professional staff.

"She had to move to Kansas City to find a job," Gauff recalled.

There were places where blacks, particularly teenage males, were not welcome. Curt Melton was uncomfortable in downtown stores.

"When we walked in all eyes were on us—security eyes," Melton recalled. "That would happen if I was in group or by myself. We could tell as black kids that white people looked at us differently."

Some neighborhoods were off-limits, not by law, but by common agreement. One of those was the predominantly Italian American St. Anne's Parish, west of Twentieth and east of Twenty-eighth streets, south of Leavenworth and north of the south Omaha viaduct. Another was the St. Francis Cabrini

Parish due east of St. Anne's. Both neighborhoods, which comprised "Little Italy," fed Central.

"The racial attitude was not good," recalled John Grandinetti, who grew up in St. Anne's. "It wasn't as bad as neighborhoods you heard about in New York or Philadelphia, but it wasn't good. We didn't have a lot of regard for black guys. The makeup of our neighborhood was purely white and not open-minded."

Grandinetti recalled being at a neighborhood recreation center on April 4, 1968, the night King was murdered in Memphis. It happened to be Grandinetti's seventeenth birthday, and he was shooting pool in the basement, when an adult supervisor approached him.

"You got a good birthday present—King's dead," the supervisor said.

Beyond Little Italy, ethnic-white, working-class neighborhoods in south Omaha were fertile for Wallace. Starting in the early 1950s, workers of Eastern European ancestry—Czechs, Poles, Croatians, and Lithuanians—had resisted the antidiscrimination efforts of their union, the United Packinghouse Workers of America (UPWA). While local leaders of Chicago's UPWA led the way in breaking down all-white plant departments and discriminatory practices in bars, restaurants, and public facilities, Omaha's local leaders held back, suspicious of a leftist agenda. Anticommunism was more rampant in Omaha than in the other major packinghouse cities (Chicago, Kansas City, East St. Louis, Milwaukee), especially among workers of Czech and Polish backgrounds, and Wallace's antileft rhetoric found a rapt audience.

Such was the racial, social, and historical context of Wallace's campaign visit to Omaha. When African Americans looked at Wallace, they saw sexual taboos, restricted real estate, and degradation. He was the whip-cracking grandee, big-bellied, squint-eyed sheriff, and sheet-wearing, cross-burning, dumb-ass goober of their nightmares.

"The Negroes see George Wallace as the personification of all that is evil in racism," the Reverend John O. McCaslin wrote in a letter to fellow priests. "I think they can bring a case for this with years of broken heads, police dogs, fire hoses, tear gas, and suppression."

And now he was in Omaha.

Two. Blocks. From. Central.

Damn.

9

Wallace for President

Dwaine Dillard barely had passed American Government as a junior, and according to one account—perhaps apocryphal—was stumped when asked if George Washington or Abraham Lincoln was the first president.

But Dillard had an ear to the street and understood that George Wallace's maverick candidacy was formidable.

"This dude is up to no good," he told friends.

Wallace's electoral math added up. He could win in the Deep South, which seemed frozen in nineteenth-century feudalism, and he might win in border states. His presence in non-southern states, such as Nebraska, could play havoc with the outcome. Neither major party was sure which would suffer the most defections to Wallace—voters from both were attracted to his anti–civil rights, pro-war rhetoric—but Wallace suspected more Democrats than Republicans would vote for him.

Even though President Johnson's popularity had plummeted, as the incumbent he still was favored—in early March—to win reelection. If Wallace won several southern and border states outright, and siphoned enough Democratic voters in northern and midwestern states, he could deny the Democrats 270 electoral votes.

Then, in return for his support, he could demand an end to federal desegregation efforts in the South and shelve the civil rights movement. It was a long shot—no presidential election had failed to produce an outright winner since 1824—but it was plausible.

Wallace was formidable, and Omahans grasped the stakes. Monday morning, at the Omaha Athletic Club, he pounded his message that "pseudo-intellectuals" advocated the destruction of the free enterprise system and wanted a Communist victory. Later he spoke to a political science class at Omaha University, which was closed to the public, but attracted about 250 protesters, including Central junior Darryl Eure, who had left school at noon. As Wallace departed the campus, Eure closed in on his car.

"I jumped on his hood and waved my placard in front of his window," Eure recalled.

Police shooed away Eure, but his appetite was whetted. Wallace's speech was scheduled for 8:00 p.m. Monday, March 4, and Eure was among the thousands who converged on the Civic Auditorium. Of the 5,400 people who attended, an estimated 500 were protesters.

One two-hundred-person group, which included students, priests, and nuns, marched over from Creighton University, behind Rev. Robert Burns and Rev. John McCaslin, who wore "Black Power—Sock It to Me" sweatshirts. McCaslin was pastor of an integrated parish on the Near North Side and director of the Catholic Social Action Office. He had been at Selma, Alabama, in 1965 when local police and Wallace's state troopers beat and hosed protest marchers.

Burns reminded his group that one of Wallace's campaign managers was Dr. Gerald Byrd, a professor of dentistry at Creighton. "(He) has given the school a black eye in the Negro community," Burns inveighed, "and we are marching tonight with our black brothers and sisters to show them that not all Bluejays share his views."

Another group came from Omaha University, organized by Marla West. A few dozen Central students were in the crowd, including Howard Rosenberg, Nancy Oostenbrug, and many of Eure's friends who later would form the militant group BUSS, among them basketball players Phil Allison, Lee Harris, and Ken Secret.

Oostenbrug and several friends made their way from Bagel with "provocative" protest signs.

"I dressed as hippielike as I could," Oostenbrug recalled.

Ray Parks recalled being home "minding my own business" when his cousin called.

"A lot of people are going to the auditorium to protest Wallace," the cousin said.

"Let's go down and see what this is," Parks replied.

Among the protesters outside the auditorium was Dillard. He had practiced with the team—which had learned it was seeded number one among the eight-team field and would play North Platte in the first round. Later, he joined the crowd in front of the auditorium but chose not to enter. Protesters marched single file around the building, chanted "We want freedom—send Wallace home," and asked people entering the rally not to sign the nominating petition.

One Central student in the building, John Gaines, was not counted among the attendees. Gaines, a burly athlete, worked on the auditorium maintenance crew and was in a utility room beneath the main floor.

Inside, most of the protesters were seated in the balcony, above the main floor. But some protesters, as they entered the building, were handed floor "delegate" passes by Wallace organizers and invited to watch from the floor. A group of about thirty protesters, mostly blacks, crowded up close to the speaker's podium—as Wallace likely intended. Even without a floor pass, Parks easily got up close to Wallace. He scaled the balcony wall, dropped eight or nine feet to the main floor, and joined the group near the podium, seated on the floor, which swelled to about fifty in the hour before Wallace appeared.

"Police told us to get back but we just stayed where we were," Parks recalled.

Wallace supporters quickly obtained more than 2,100 signatures—750 were needed to certify him as a third-party candidate on the primary ballot. At about 9:00 p.m. Wallace stepped onto the podium and tried to speak, but was drowned out by jeers throughout the arena. Protesters in front of the podium tossed small wooden sticks and cardboard—from their signs—at the rostrum.

Police lined up in front of the podium and faced the protesters.

"These are the free-speech folks, you know," Wallace said. "And these are the kind of folks the people in this country are sick and tired of."

Wallace pounded the podium as his supporters roared in approval. Protesters threw more debris at the podium. Wallace

Protesters jeered and hurled debris at George Wallace. Reprinted with permission of the *Omaha World-Herald*.

thanked his supporters for putting him on the ballot, and continued, "I have never in my life made a statement that would reflect upon anybody because of race or color, creed or religion, and I don't intend to do so tonight."

Noise from protesters mounted, Wallace blamed the "breakdown of law and order" on the usual suspects, and then struggled to speak over the noise. He shouted, "Would you all like to stay or not?"

Somebody on the podium, possibly Wallace, said, "Call in the police now." Two of Wallace's bodyguards moved to the row of officers and whispered to two of them.

Police moved to clear the aisle in front of the podium, at which point Wallace shouted, "Ladies and gentlemen, I want to say that you ought to be thankful for the police of Omaha."

George Wallace eyeballed a heckler: "Why don't you get out of here. Get him out of here." Reprinted with permission of the *Omaha World-Herald*.

He eyeballed a heckler and said, "Why don't you get out of here. Get him out of here."

Accounts differ as to what happened next.

Police ordered a nineteen-year-old black man to move aside, and according to the *World-Herald*, he swung at them. Police responded with a "flying wedge" that drove forward and "swept the dissenters the length of the Arena floor and out the door."

But an account provided by the alternative newspaper the *Buffalo Chip* was different. It reported that after Wallace's "free-speech" remark, a plainclothes officer

grabbed his pressurized can of Mace and shot in a wide arc into the group of demonstrators. The Mace attack started an instantaneous chain of events.

The unarmed demonstrators turned to flee, and the police followed them, beating them on the back of the head as they ran. As

Omaha police routed protesters with clubs and Mace. Reprinted
with permission of the *Omaha World-Herald*.

*the demonstrators tried to escape, people picked up folding chairs
and beat them as they ran by, or threw chairs at them.*

*There was no attempt made by Wallace to calm the crowd
or stop the police once it was clear that the demonstrators were
leaving. Instead, his words incited the riot, and Mr. Wallace stood
on the podium with a little smile on his face.*

An account in the *Creightonian*, the Creighton student newspaper, placed culpability on police and Wallace supporters,
as had the *Buffalo Chip*. Claude Broomes, a black freshman,
said,

A Negro in front of me jumped up to holler at Wallace and was pushed into a cop who knocked him down. The kid got up to defend himself, then everybody jumped up and police naturally pushed them back then drew night sticks. Next thing I knew I was getting run over. I bumped into a cop who sprayed me with Mace. Mace. Then I threw up my hands and turned to run down the aisle. A cop hit me on the back of the head. I put my hand over my head to protect myself. I got hit by chairs all the way out.

Parks's recollection supported the first account. "The cops started at the back of the crowd (of protesters) and told people to move—I was at the front," he recalled. "They got to the last guy in front of me, and brushed his leg, and this dumb ass jumped up and took a swing, and the police jumped on him, and they all crawled over me. Then everybody jumped up and all hell broke loose. Police were billy-clubbing everybody around me. One cop grabbed me and let me go. Somebody spun me around and I had Mace in my eye."

From the balcony, Eure, Graves, White, and Oostenbrug watched in disbelief. As the protesters were driven from the podium, Eure recalled, "chairs started flying." Nancy Oostenbrug recalled that fleeing protesters were "being hit with metal folding chairs until the chairs broke."

Hayden West also watched from the balcony.

"My sister was in the middle aisle with fifteen or twenty people," he recalled. "Then all hell broke loose."

Protesters, chased by police, ran the gauntlet to the rear exit, pummeled by Wallace supporters, who punched, kicked, and threw chairs. One officer hit a protester who was held by a Wallace supporter. One protester, on his hands and knees,

Omaha police drove protesters from the main floor of the Civic Auditorium. Reprinted with permission of the *Omaha World-Herald*.

was hit over the back with a folding chair. Once or twice an officer protected a protester.

A woman with a bloodied head and two young children made her way down a ramp toward the utility room where student John Gaines worked. Gaines sat her down, put a paper towel to her wound, and ran up the ramp for help. What he saw astonished him.

"Three of four cops were pounding on somebody, and in another direction people were pounding on a cop," Gaines recalled.

The protesters on the balcony level rushed to the lobby on the ground floor and found themselves under assault from police and Wallace supporters. An officer brandished his nightstick in front of White, who froze, and returned his stare.

"It was a stalemate—he knew I hadn't done anything," White recalled.

The officer relented and moved on, and White got out of the building unharmed. Outside, White saw the sidewalks fill up.

"It was like letting air out of a balloon—people exploded out of the auditorium," White recalled.

Eure and Graves made it out to the street—unscathed—and surveyed the scene. Parks, watery-eyed from the Mace, did the same.

"People were laying on the sidewalk all bloodied up," Parks recalled.

Oostenbrug and a friend ran to a hotel near the auditorium that was managed by her friend's father.

"We went there to get wet paper towels to pat our eyes," Oostenbrug recalled.

Eure recalled that David L. Rice, an acolyte of Father McCaslin's progressive ministry, and a contributor to the *Buffalo Chip*, was bloodied.

"They beat the spit out of David," Eure said.

Another Central student, Jo Anne Donaldson, had made it outside when a *World-Herald* reporter asked her a question.

Donaldson screamed, "You're going to get it, baby, just you wait. You're going to get it this summer. Heat, baby, heat."

She continued: "He's going to split this country apart—Nebraska's going to be a ball of fire this summer. It's going to be the hottest state there is.

"They're going to blame us—but he's going to do it—not us."

Anger escalated outside. The *Buffalo Chip* reported that "angry Negroes tore up pieces of pavement, bashed in several car windshields, and broke windows of the auditorium."

Inside, glass rained down on Gaines from a window shattered by a rock, and he sought refuge with other employees in a secured room. Minutes later he decided to wade into the melee on the side of the police.

"Cops were getting beaten up—I helped them if they were outnumbered," Gaines recalled.

Groups of blacks left the auditorium and turned up Twentieth Street toward the Near North Side. Eure and Graves found a ride with Phil Allison, and as they drove north on Twentieth Street they saw unusual activity. Hundreds of blacks were in the streets, in unseasonable fifty-degree weather, aroused by news reports of the violent melee.

Rev. R. F. Jenkins, a civil rights leader, described the scene in the documentary *Street of Dreams*: "They began to run, and they began to run north, and after they ran for a distance, the decided to stop and do something. Not run, but burn."

Crowds turned into mobs. Four white motorists driving on North Twenty-fourth Street were attacked and beaten, and nine other persons were injured. Storefront windows were broken, ten businesses were looted, and buildings were set afire. Sadie's Home Bakery, at Twenty-fourth and Binney, was not damaged because John Biddle, his parents, and siblings had surrounded it.

"We stayed right there—that was our livelihood," Biddle recalled.

Not the best way to rest up for the state tournament, three days hence, but for Biddle the family business came first.

A sixteen-year-old African American boy was killed by an off-duty white cop at the Crosstown Pawn Shop. Reprinted with permission of the *Omaha World-Herald*.

This was America's first racial disturbance of 1968, and soon it took a tragic turn. At about 3:00 a.m., Tuesday, a young black man, Howard Stevenson, was killed as he allegedly tried to crawl through the broken window of a pawnshop on North Twenty-fourth Street. Stevenson, sixteen, who had dropped out of Tech High, was shot by a white off-duty Omaha cop, James Abbott, who had been hired to guard the shop. Abbott fired one shot from his 12-gauge riot gun. No warning shot was fired, and self-defense was not a factor.

Stevenson's death led the Tuesday morning news, and students heard of it as they readied for school. Anger coalesced on the Near North Side. Police were accused of excessive force at the rally, and Stevenson's shooting was instantly suspect as brutal and excessive. As one black leader said later, "The penalty for looting is not death." Many black students arrived at

Central in agitation. Some gathered at the "sacred C," inside the west entrance, in full-throated belligerence, and stepped on it, tradition be damned.

"There was a lot of acting out before school—a lot of yelling in the halls," Dan Daly recalled.

Others refused to enter the building. They gathered on the west side, just off the property, held signs, and chanted, "Black Power." White students who parked in a lot west of school picked their way through this angry cordon—gingerly—to reach the west entrance.

Larry Cain watched events unfold from a window in room 232, his homeroom, which was the classroom of his father, Bob Cain, who taught English.

"My dad and I had a clear view of the (mostly black) students standing in mass on the street between Central and Joslyn Museum," Cain recalled.

Several black administrators from Omaha Public Schools headquarters arrived to negotiate with the protesting students. In animated discussions, administrators pleaded with students to attend classes, and students defended their right to boycott. Some black students relented and entered school, but the majority held their ground.

"The students literally turned their back on them," Cain recalled.

Inside the building the agitation of black students increased and tensions between black and white students mounted. Cain recalled being in a library study hall, supervised by Catherine Blanchard, when a group of black students entered—Dillard among them—and thrust their fists into the air. They shouted "Black Power," at which point several black students seated in the study hall arose, and joined in the chant. When the group of intruders left, the black students who had been seated followed them out.

"As they went down the hall they were gathering in size," Cain recalled.

Dillard's presence in the group stopped Cain cold. He had met Dillard two-and-a-half years earlier, as a sophomore, in a gym class. As a squad leader, Cain was asked to introduce Dillard, a new transfer, to members of the class. Dillard's most striking quality was his friendliness and ability to get along with almost everybody, Cain observed. Now Cain thought Dillard had changed. His basketball stardom had made him a different person.

"I felt he was thrown into a spotlight of helping lead students in protest," Cain recalled.

Later that morning Ray Parks saw Dillard on a landing halfway up one of the boys' stairways. Dillard stood over a trashcan that had been pulled out of a restroom. He lit a match, dropped it in, and watched the trash can go up in flames. Then he sauntered off.

Tom Milder recalled that Dillard came in late to a music class and hid behind a pillar as the instructor, Calvin Carlson, spoke from the stage. When Carlson turned away, Dillard stepped out from the pillar and rifled a stale hamburger bun, which whistled past his face.

"Dwaine made that funny face he made," Milder recalled. "Then he was out the door."

By midday some white students — in tears — had left school. Some decided that it was unsafe to stay. Panicked parents, who had heard dire news reports, pulled out others. White students with cars parked west of the school had to walk through a cordon of black protesters, some of which, at this point, were not Central students. One of those white students was Gary Soiref, sports editor of the *Register*.

"It was tense," Soiref recalled. "A black guy I knew helped me get through."

Vince Orduna and Marlyn Jackson helped Bonnie Knight and her white girlfriends get through the cordon to the parking lot.

"I was not afraid, but Vince and Marlyn were," Knight recalled.

Teachers monitored the halls with apprehension, unsure of when to exercise authority, and how much. Nelson, the creaky demoralized principal, was holed up in his office.

"We felt he wasn't in charge," recalled Mike Gaherty, the journalism teacher.

Moller, the assistant principal, had gone to Lincoln that morning to work on his doctorate. He returned at midday after he had gotten word of the problems, and assisted Cliff Dale, the other assistant principal. Moller and Dale tried to assert control in the hallways and classrooms, but events had snowballed. In the afternoon, skirmishes broke out between black and white students, primarily white members of the football team. The problem began when black students chanted, "Umgawa, Black Power," and some whites responded with, "Umgawa, White Power."

"The issue that came up was who was tougher—who was running the school?" recalled Delmar Givehand.

Assistant Principal Gaylord Moller tried to keep peace in
Central's hallways. Reprinted with permission of the *Omaha
Central High School O-Book*.

In the middle of the action were a brawny sophomore football player and wrestler, Tom Vincentini, who grew up in St.
Francis Cabrini Parish, and his older brother, Pete Vincentini,
a senior football player. Their group included John Gaines,
Frank Digilio, and John Arman.

Tom Vincentini's "physical strength and toughness was way
beyond anything I grew up with," recalled John Grandinetti.

Later, Grandinetti came to know Vincentini and enjoy his
friendship. But in March 1968, "he was a tough kid I didn't
want any piece of," Grandinetti recalled.

Darryl Eure, a wrestling teammate of Vincentini, recalled
that Vincentini threatened him when he saw that Eure was a protester. Eure mentioned the threat to his friend Lee Harris.

"Lee wanted to jump Vincentini," Eure recalled. "The atmosphere was bad—if you had lit a match it probably would have burnt us all up."

Gaines recalled that black students tried to intimidate him.

"You had seven or eight guys walking down a hallway and they expected you to dodge into classrooms or stairways to get out of their way," Gaines recalled. "I wasn't programmed that way. Somebody would give me an elbow and a fist fight would start."

When the last bell rang at 3:15 p.m., a group of black and white males met outside, close to the gym, on the northwest side. A fight broke out, involving Dillard, Ken Secret, the Vincentini brothers, and a few others.

"We passed a few blows," Secret recalled.

Basketball practice was scheduled to start in a few minutes. But Dillard, and other players—Phil Allison and Lee Harris—were otherwise occupied. Two players, Harvey Josin and Ralph Hackney, watched the fight from a window at the side of the gym.

"A bunch of black guys whaled on one of the Vincentinis, and then it was over—it didn't last long," Josin recalled.

Richard Jones, a boys' counselor, broke up the fight, Secret recalled. Dillard ambled in to practice and turned his attention to basketball. Marquiss, the coach, seemed oblivious to Dillard's behavior off the court. Two practices remained before the first round of the state tournament—Marquiss was determined to block out distractions.

Yet, when Marquiss drove home, his car was pelted with rocks on Radial Highway.

As the sun set on Tuesday, the impact of Wallace's visit was assessed by stunned law enforcement and school officials. More than half of the students at Central, Tech, and North high schools, and at Horace Mann Junior High, had stayed out or had left early. More than fifty windows were broken at Horace Mann, where students calmed down only after Ernie Chambers told them, "You are putting on a show for the crackers—don't let them make a show out of you." Incidents of student vandalism were reported throughout the Near North Side. Police reported seventeen injured persons, twenty-seven damaged autos, ten looted stores, and six vandalized buildings. Homemade firebombs exploded inside several damaged buildings.

Fear enveloped the city. "No school was immune—even the all-white Westside and Burke high schools were rife with rumors that "they" were coming to get white students," reported Sun Newspapers of Omaha.

Underlying the violence was an anger described by a black activist, David L. Rice, in the *Buffalo Chip*:

This is Tuesday night. It is 11:30. Outside, the police are cruising up and down streets and alleys. Some minutes ago I got back home from 24th Street. While I was there I talked with many friends and other people whom I did not know. For 15 minutes I remained on the lot at 24th and Lake. Many of us discussed the question of which area of the city should receive the bulk of our payment for "services" given us by the Omaha Police Department and their ignorant supporters Monday night. Others talked about looking forward to killing or beating hell out of whitey. By the time you read this article, homes burned to the ground might be black upon West Omaha soil. By the time you read this article, how many will have died? Why is this happening? It might be good to ask the Omaha Police or our city officials, or the fat bigots who remain asses sitting upon their asses.

. . . I am very tired now. And it's getting late. As I prepare to retire to the bed, I consider the animal activities of the Omaha Police Department, the unabashed lying of our news media, and the unlimited stupidity of Mayor (A. V.) Sorensen. And I hope that the metal Citizens' Protection sticks, which I am passing out, will help the police get the kind of justice they have asked for.

Dollis penned her diary account with equal agitation:

I thought things were bad yesterday! Last night a racist presidential candidate, George Wallace from Alabama, talked at the civic auditorium. A bunch of Negro kids got pushed around and hit with chairs, and then later that night a Negro boy was shot and killed because he was looting a store. So all day in school the colored kids were yelling "Black Power" and Dwaine got in two fights. There were threats of riots so all the white kids were dismissed to go home. But I'm not afraid so I stayed all day. What I'm really afraid is that Dwaine or some of the team will get kicked out of school and not be able to play in the state tournament. And what really hurts is that Willie isn't talking to me, and some colored kids ignore me now because I'm white.

Wallace was gone—he had flown out after his rally. The Omaha he left behind was in pain. High school basketball seemed irrelevant, but only for a moment.

10

Darkness, Darkness

Police booked him as "Dwyaine Rufus Dillard." He was arrested at 3922 North Nineteenth Street and charged with "suspicion of possession of Molotov Cocktails." The report stated: "The above party arrested in connection with having bricks and Molotov cocktails in the auto he was riding in."

The report did not state, "Basketball star invites chaos upon his school, teammates, coach, state basketball tournament, and presidential campaign," but it might well have.

His employer was listed as "Central High" and his occupation as "student." His grandmother's address, 4116 North Twenty-third Street, was listed as his home. The report described him as six feet seven, 195 pounds, with brown eyes, black hair, dark complexion, and no scars. He was identified as an American citizen, eighteen, single, with no sickness or injury.

Dillard was in a car with five other black males when police stopped it at around 11:30 p.m., Tuesday. Nathaniel Goodwin, twenty-six, was the owner and driver of the '66 blue Rambler sedan. The others were Calvin Brown, seventeen; Lloyd Brown, twenty-one; Calvin Webster, eighteen; and David Russ III, sixteen.

A court document gave this account:

On the evening of March 5, 1968, three officers in a police cruiser were watching for possible attempts to start fires on the north side in Omaha when they were alerted to be on the lookout for a car which had been seen in the vicinity of an earlier fire. They observed a car answering the description given and immediately started to pursue it. The car pulled to the curb and came to a stop when the cruiser was approximately 50 feet away. The cruiser drove to within 4 to 5 feet of the stopped car. During that interval the officers observed the right rear door of the car come partially open and a brown paper sack come out of the car. One of the officers also observed the throwing of a silver object from the front window on the driver's side. After the cruiser stopped, the defendant, who was the owner and driver of the car, came back to the cruiser.

The sack which was found near the car contained three liquor bottles filled with a liquid described as ethylene dichloride and diethyl lead, a highly inflammable and explosive material. The silver object was identified as a bottle with a rag sticking out of the top, filled with the same liquid, which the officers testified smelled like gasoline and which they described as a Molotov cocktail. The officers also found a large number of rocks on the floor board on both sides of the rear seat.

Those were the facts, according to police. But there were unanswered questions, some of which concerned Dillard's actions and culpability. Why was he in a car with firebombs and rocks, before midnight, one day after the Wallace rally, and two days before the state tournament?

The next day Dillard provided Marquiss an explanation: He and Calvin Webster, a friend, had spent the evening playing basketball and socializing at the outdoor Bryant courts. When they left to walk home, Goodwin drove past and offered them a ride. Lloyd Brown, Calvin Brown, and Russ also were offered a ride. They were passengers for no more than two blocks before police stopped the car.

"Coach, I was not involved in this—I did not throw any Molotov cocktails—I would not do it," Dillard said. "I don't know what the other guys in the car were doing."

Goodwin later testified that he had spent Tuesday evening with his girlfriend, and at 11:00 p.m. had gone to get a beer at Twenty-fourth and Lake streets. He saw Dillard and Webster and offered them a ride, and they slid into his front seat. He also picked up the other three, who asked for a ride and piled into the back seat. Goodwin said that they "rode around for awhile" but did not stop until police pulled them over shortly after midnight. Goodwin testified that he had no knowledge of firebombs allegedly found outside the car, or of rocks found on the floor of the backseat. He also testified that he had seen nothing thrown from the car, and that the firebombs and rocks cited by police had not been in his car before he picked up his passengers.

Goodwin's car was searched at the antiquated police headquarters downtown, at Eleventh and Douglas. A loaded .32-caliber handgun—unregistered—was found in the locked glove compartment. Goodwin testified that the gun belonged to his father, had been in the car for over a year, and that he carried it for protection in his part-time job for a delivery service.

Webster and Dillard had played basketball at the outdoor Bryant Center courts before they hitched a ride with Goodwin.

"We got a ride from Nate, and at Eighteenth and Sprague we saw the police coming," Webster recalled. "We could have run but we hadn't done anything. We weren't going to run—they might shoot us.

"They called us the N-word and told us to get out of the car. We said we hadn't done anything. They saw Dwaine—I think they recognized him. Dwaine said, 'We ain't gotta do nothing,' and then an officer hit him with the butt of a gun. One cop said, 'You want to run, nigger, go ahead and run.' Nobody moved.

"There were no firebombs—the police made up that story. They looked around the car and didn't find anything."

Webster recalled that the police handcuffed him, as well as Dillard, and the other four, and transported them to headquarters in a couple of cruisers.

Calvin Brown also had played basketball at the Bryant Center that evening. Brown played for Tech, which had advanced to the state tournament. He had met up with Lloyd Brown and Russ before Goodwin offered them a ride.

After Goodwin's car was stopped, in Brown's recollection, police ordered the occupants spread-eagled against the police cruiser.

"I asked them why we were jacked up like this—what did we do wrong?" Brown recalled. "They told us to shut up and said we'd get shot if we moved. They talked real nasty and treated us pretty rough.

"Then they searched the trunk—we couldn't actually see what was going on because the trunk was open. They said they found all these firebombs. We didn't know what was in the trunk—and we indicated that to the police officers.

"They handcuffed us and took us downtown and inter-
rogated us. We told them the same thing—we didn't know
what was in the trunk."

Goodwin's recollection was that when he saw a police cruiser
behind him on Twenty-fourth Street, he drove to Nineteenth
before he pulled over.

"One guy yelled 'Don't stop,'" Goodwin recalled. "I said
'Why?' He said, 'I got a package.'

"I stopped and they all got out of the car. But I was held
accountable for what they found in the package."

Ray Schulte was one of three arresting officers—each
white—along with Harley Godberson and Robert Wiese.
Goodwin's car was stopped, Schulte remembered, "because
they were suspicious parties driving down the street—we pulled
'em over as a general check." Dillard was unknown to the officers until he produced identification, at which point he was
cooperative, "and seemed like a nice kid."

For the six young men arrested, the specter of being jailed
must have been frightening. A wide gulf of mistrust existed
between the mostly black Near North Side and the mostly
white Omaha police force. "They had the reputation where
they would literally kick your butts—beat you up first and
ask questions later," remembered Calvin Brown.

Ernie Chambers's recollection was that Omaha's racial cli-
mate was "very bad, mainly because of police harassment of
and hounding of black people."

Mayor A. V. Sorensen, who held office from 1965 to 1969,
said of the police, in a 1977 interview, "Their procedure was
to use their clubs at the slightest provocation."

Police headquarters featured an elevator that transported suspects from the garage to the fourth-floor booking area. The elevator was infamous in Near North Side lore—it was said to be where black suspects were roughed up—and where bloodstains were removed with periodic scrubbings.

Father McCaslin, director of the Catholic Social Action Office and perhaps the most trusted white man on the Near North Side, described Omaha police as "trigger-happy bigots" in a letter to fellow priests later in March. McCaslin wrote that police engaged in "improper enforcement of laws mixed with petty police harassment and not so petty police brutality—by this I mean the police take payoffs on gambling, liquor, and prostitution while at the same time use improper language and denial of rights, especially of young people, through constant harassment."

Black males in cars often were stopped because they were black, and therefore suspicious—a practice not yet known as racial profiling. Delmar Givehand remembered when Bruce Mitchell bought an old car and invited him for a ride. Givehand suggested they drive to Bagel.

"No, we'll get stopped," said Mitchell.

"No we won't."

Sure enough, as Mitchell drove west across Forty-fifth Street, police pulled him over, and he glared at Givehand.

"I told you so."

Goodwin recollected that in the weeks prior to his arrest he had frequented an apartment building in west Omaha where he socialized with a group of white nurses. He believed those visits caused his car to come under police surveillance.

Mixed signals from city hall muddled black-police relations. After the 1966 disorders, Sorensen held out an olive branch when he fired a top police official, who had labeled the Near North Side a "jungle" and had insisted on aggressive and hard-nosed tactics.

Yet Sorensen praised police for performing "superbly" at the Wallace rally and blamed the violence on the two "militant" priests, McCaslin and Burns, who were charged with disorderly conduct. Three months later Sorensen shot down a proposal for civilian oversight of police and echoed Wallace when he said that racial tension could be traced to "inflammatory statements and activities of the very militant Negro, whose primary mission seems to be to foster tensions between the races and to make headlines." Another Wallace echo was heard when Sorensen said, "In Omaha and America . . . we need to weep a little less for the hoodlum and criminal and cheer a little more for the job being done by the police officers everywhere."

Schulte, a south Omaha native, father of two young children, and a six-year veteran of the force, had experience as a white cop in a black neighborhood. Not long before, he had been sent to a housing project near North Twenty-fourth Street, where gunfire had been reported. It was dark, and as he walked around a building a black man jumped from the shadows and stuck a gun in his belly. The man pulled the trigger, but the gun jammed. A chase ensued, and the man was lost in a crowd on North Twenty-fourth. Later, Schulte, not a religious man, said "a few prayers."

He remembered the incident with a hint of amazement, and noted that by comparison, Dillard's arrest was routine.

"Let me tell you one thing—90 percent of those colored people were straight shooters," Schulte recalled. "You had that 10-percent crowd just like the white people—they wanted to defy the law and do things their way. I didn't have any problem with the residents down there—I got along good with them."

Schulte rode with Dillard and the others down to headquarters, entered through the garage off Eleventh Street, walked down a hallway, and rode the elevator up to the fourth floor. Nothing improper occurred, and everybody was booked and fingerprinted by 2:20 a.m.

A newspaper photographer snapped a shot of Schulte delivering the evidence—described as "one pint bottle gasoline in Thunderbird Wine bottle, half-pint bottle gasoline in Seagram's V. O. Whisky bottle, half-pint bottle gasoline in Windsor Canadian Whisky bottle, clear bottle quarter-filled with gasoline with rag in top"—at headquarters. The photo ran the next afternoon.

In the morning Phyllis Briggs, accompanied by her minister, Herbert Robinson, came to get her son out of jail. Ernie Chambers was at police headquarters as well—his nephew was the youngest passenger, David Russ. But Chambers's primary concern was Howard Stevenson, the teenager shot to death by the off-duty cop, James Abbott, in the looting that followed Wallace's speech.

"The cop who shot him had a bad reputation—I wanted some answers," Chambers recalled.

Chambers, for the moment, turned his attention to his nephew and Dillard. Briggs was ushered into Dillard's cell, and in a glance she knew he was embarrassed.

"You mad?" Dillard asked.

Briggs smacked him upside the head and scolded him for being "a follower." He wept.

"You need to listen and think," she said.

Chambers talked with Municipal Judge Paul Hickman and County Attorney Donald "Pinky" Knowles, who wanted assurance that Dillard, if released, would appear in court for a March 20 hearing.

"Let him out and I'll make sure he's here," Chambers said. "I can guarantee that better than a bondsman."

Dillard was released without bond and left with his mother. She pressed him for an explanation, and what she heard differed from what he later told Marquiss, and from Webster's account.

"He said he was asleep, and they came and got him out of bed and he followed," Briggs recalled. "Then they went to find George Wallace and crucify him."

The *World-Herald* "sunrise edition" reported the arrest of six men but not their names. It reported a second night of disturbances: three more persons were injured, another store was looted, twelve more autos were damaged, and six more buildings were vandalized.

Local radio and TV stations reported Dillard's arrest during the morning commute, and students arrived at Central in disbelief. For the second consecutive day black students boycotted, though fewer than the day before, and assembled outside. Overall attendance was off about 60 percent. But as word of Dillard's arrest circulated through the deserted hallways, the boycott seemed like yesterday's news.

Marquiss learned of the arrest from TV news before he left for work.

"Dad was stunned," Jim Marquiss recalled.

The rest of the day did not provide him much chance to recover. That morning school and city officials met to decide whether two nights of civil disorder in Omaha was reason enough to move the Class A basketball tournament to Lincoln. Safety concerns had escalated, especially with outstate schools—North Platte, Hastings, and Columbus—in the tournament. Omaha Mayor A. V. Sorensen voiced concern that the Civic Auditorium, the site of Wallace's rally, would be a lightning rod for protestors. The high school sports governing body considered postponing the tournament for a week, playing the games in Omaha in the mornings, and outright canceling the tournament. But ultimately it decided to move the tournament to Lincoln, and to play most of the games at 9:30 a.m., for security reasons.

The sudden shift in tournament logistics occurred as Marquiss dealt with Dillard. A spontaneous debate erupted over his status on Central's team, and Marquiss was at the center of it. Nelson, the principal, told Marquiss he wanted Dillard off the team. Talk-radio commentators reported a deluge of calls from outraged listeners who demanded Dillard's ouster from the tournament. Don Lee, the sportswriter, let Marquiss know that the newspaper was experiencing the same phenomenon with its readers.

"What Dad heard over and over was that Dillard was a felon and a thug and didn't deserve to be playing for Central," recalled Jim Marquiss.

World-Herald sports columnist Wally Provost described the situation a few days later:

Dillard was not just another boy in trouble. He was a Symbol.

To some people he was an accused criminal who should be dealt with firmly and promptly. He symbolized all that they feared from lawlessness.

To another faction he was a school athletic hero, perhaps even an idolized rebel.

Considering the extreme emotions of the city, this was a hot one; anybody who touched it could expect to get burned.

Marquiss, who had taken Dillard at his word and believed him innocent, argued that Dillard should not be punished until his case was heard. He made his point with Nelson and the superintendent of schools, Dr. Owen Knutzen.

"You cannot convict and punish the kid before he has a fair and legal trial," Marquiss insisted.

Both Knutzen and Nelson held power over Dillard. Eligibility rules empowered them to suspend any student athlete "who because of bad habits or improper conduct would not represent the school in a becoming manner."

As much as Knutzen and Nelson wanted Dillard off the team, neither wanted to make the decision—and risk a political firestorm. Finally they decided that Marquiss should decide.

"Anyhow, the burden was dropped on Coach Marquiss," Provost wrote. "The buck had been passed the full route."

Dillard missed the afternoon practice. Afterward, Marquiss told reporters he still was on the team, and that "the only thing I'll say is that he is a bona fide Central High student and that the administration made the decision."

But whether Dillard would play still was in question. Though Marquiss had opposed premature "conviction," he wrestled with the issue of discipline, a nuance that reflected his moral compass and years of teaching and coaching. Dillard may or may not have been criminal, but he had not acted in the best interest of his team. As Marquiss parsed the situation, he told reporters he had not decided if Dillard would play.

Late in the afternoon Chambers was at Central with a message for Marquiss, which he delivered to Jim Martin, the junior varsity coach.

"I vouched for Dillard," Chambers said. "Keep him in line."

As the sun set Wednesday evening, Dillard's sensational story hit the national TV newscasts. Omahans arriving home from work and school saw Dillard's arrest covered nationally by Walter Cronkite (CBS) and Huntley and Brinkley (NBC). The newspaper evening edition ran a front-page photo of Dillard at the police station.

When Marquiss went home that evening, his telephone rang over and over. Some calls were from school officials, but most were random from people "in the community" who had strong opinions about Dillard. As the calls continued, Marquiss had his wife and sons screen them.

"People were yelling and screaming and threatening," recalled Don Marquiss.

After hanging up on a few callers, Marquiss ordered the phones disconnected. The evening was well on, and he was worn out. As he readied for bed, his oldest son noticed a "flash" outside a front window. When Jim Marquiss looked out he was stunned.

"Dad, you better come look."

The coach and his son ran outside to find "two or three" wooden crosses burning in their front yard. They threw water on the flames and knocked down the crosses, which singed the grass. Jim Marquiss was amazed Dillard had aroused such feelings, and that the crosses were hammered so firmly into the ground. He saw his father tremble with anger and waited for his explosion.

But Marquiss gathered himself and turned to go in.

"This may not be the end of it," he said.

Across town, with darkness her pillow, Dollis wrote: "Just what everyone was afraid of happened. Dwaine got arrested last night for possession of a gun, bricks, and bombs. He was in jail because it is a felony, but they announced on the news that he was released and innocent till proven guilty. So he can still play for the state tournament. After that who cares what happens to him."

11

The Broken Hearted

Thursday morning broke clear and mild and nothing like the storm in Steve Moss's soul. As Dillard and teammates, with overnight bags, piled on to the bus outside Central, Moss pulled Marquiss aside.

"I'm not going," Moss said.

The senior guard explained that he could not play given the events of the last three days. Marquiss urged him to reconsider—Moss was his second or third player off the bench, and Marquiss knew something that would make Moss's presence vital.

"This isn't about basketball," Moss said. "I can't go to Lincoln."

Moss's decision, he explained, was his personal protest over Wallace and disorder in his neighborhood. He had not tried to influence his teammates, or even his brother, Jerry, a junior guard. The final straw had been the transfer of the tournament to Lincoln.

"It's an insult," Moss said. "To me and every black person in Omaha."

Privately, Moss harbored resentment against Marquiss, or what he thought Marquiss stood for. It stemmed partially from his disappointment with how Marquiss had used him — off the bench. But it also had to do with Moss's activist perception of race and sports, as articulated by Harry Edwards.

Viewed through Edwards's prism, Marquiss exploited his black players. And not only Marquiss — the Central High administration and the Nebraska School Activities Association did as well. The deconstructed view of Dillard, for instance, was that he was used as an athlete at the expense of his academics.

"We were being pimped — it pissed me off," Moss recalled, "I felt like Marquiss was a pimp. I had no real animosity toward him personally — he was part of the times."

When the bus pulled away from Central, Moss was not on it. His teammates, already subdued by recent events, were further sobered to hear he had quit. Gloom descended, as the bus began the one-hour journey to Lincoln. Nobody could think of what to say, until one of the managers, Mike Sherman, broke the silence.

"Hey Dwaine, where's your ball and chain?"

Dillard chuckled, and in an instant his teammates rocked with hilarity. They loosened up for the rest of the journey, and were in high spirits when they arrived at Pershing Auditorium in downtown Lincoln, an hour before their 9:30 game against North Platte. But their mood soon nosedived. As they suited up Marquiss announced that Dillard would not play — he was to be benched as punishment for violation of training rules Tuesday night.

"He was out too late — the rules apply to everybody," Marquiss said.

Dillard was nonplussed, but his closest teammates reacted in anger, led by Frazier, whose role was not without cause. Frazier had nursed a race-related grievance since the previous fall, when, as a disciplinary action, the football coach had demoted him to backup quarterback, behind a white teammate, Don Riemer.

Now Frazier's resentment surfaced on Dillard's behalf. He suggested a boycott, unless Dillard were allowed to play, and the idea took on life. Frazier told Marquiss the team wished to take a vote, and asked that he and Jim Martin, the junior varsity coach, leave the locker room. Marquiss agreed, to Martin's amazement.

"Warren, they have to play," Martin protested.

"It's okay. Let them vote."

The two coaches exited and the players voted. A few minutes later Marquiss and Martin reentered the locker room. Frazier stood up.

"We're not playing," he said.

Marquiss snapped.

"Get out there!"

Startled and cowed, the players jumped up and ran out of the locker room, Frazier among them. They ran onto the court with as much verve as could be mustered at the unusual hour of 9:30 a.m., and their attention turned to the game at hand.

Two dozen helmeted state troopers and Lincoln police, as well as a police dog, ringed the court and took positions high in the stands. Assistant principals Gaylord Moller and Cliff Dale, and several young Central teachers—Dan Daly, Charles Funkhouser, Richard Butolph, and Brian Watson—took positions on the floor facing the crowd, as per order of Nelson.

"We were supposed to keep the crowd from overreacting and from acting negatively toward Dwaine," Daly recalled.

The crowd of one thousand included only about four hundred mostly white Central students who had driven or found rides to Lincoln—no buses had been arranged. At least half the crowd was from North Platte, a small town in southwest Nebraska.

Dillard, in uniform, sat next to Marquiss on the bench. Henry Caruthers, a five-foot-eleven junior guard, was the fifth starter. Hunter, despite a bruised instep, jumped center in place of Dillard. Griffin, with a mild ankle sprain, and Biddle were in their normal positions.

Frazier was in his normal spot as well, though banged up from a recent game of touch football. But he had more on his mind—Sue Glyn's pregnancy soon would be apparent. She continued to profess her love, even as he saw Dollis.

The night before, Dollis had stopped over to his house. She wrote:

Tonite I ate dinner with Susie and Marilyn Katz and Susie took me over to Willie's on the way home! I've been dying not talking to him but now everything is really happy! He is so cute and funny! He was washing dishes and sweeping the floor with a little yellow apron on. I laughed so hard—he's so big and he was cleaning the kitchen! But he can really kiss good.

Still emotional about Dillard's punishment, seething with resentment, perhaps unsettled by Glyn, and inspired by Dollis, Frazier played the game of his high school career. He led all scorers with twenty points and grabbed twelve rebounds in a 70–51 win over North Platte.

Marquiss benched Dillard against first-round opponent North Platte. Reprinted with permission of the *Omaha World-Herald*.

Conde Sargent wrote that Frazier "went to the post" in leading the Dillard-less Eagles. Shorter than three North Platte starters, Frazier poured in seven jump shots from near the free-throw line, and hit all six of his foul shots. Central led 30–21 at half and finished off North Platte with a 22–15 fourth quarter.

Caruthers justified his insertion in the lineup with ten points and eight rebounds. Hunter scored sixteen, Biddle twelve, and Griffin eight in a balanced attack.

Throughout the game photographers hovered near the Central bench and close to Dillard. Though Marquiss had a no-interview embargo on all of his players, a photographer asked Dillard a question as play proceeded, and Marquiss shooed him away.

After the final buzzer Dillard, relieved and pleased, rushed to his teammates on the court, congratulated them, and exchanged "skin." To media, Marquiss praised Caruthers and voiced satisfaction with the balanced effort. "We never play with one man—I'm real satisfied with the kids," he said.

The game was without incident on the court and in the stands, a fact reported in the evening edition as the lead story. Under the headline "Lincoln Police Guard Courts as Basket Ball Tourney Opens," the newspaper ran a photo of Marquiss and Dillard, at the end of the bench, intent on the game.

The same story reported that Marquiss had not said whether Dillard would play in the semifinal round. Victories by Boys Town, Omaha Tech, and Lincoln Northeast had set up semifinal pairings of Central–Boys Town, and Tech-Northeast. Boys Town, state champion in 1965 and 1966, had lost to Central by one point in the season opener, but had fallen by twelve at midseason.

By this time, the Near North Side had quieted, as a group of sixty clergy and community leaders walked the neighborhoods, and five plainclothes police officers went into schools and churches to ask for calm.

Thursday evening the team quartered on campus at a university dorm. Dillard had energy to burn, and may have seen no point in conserving it, in view of his uncertain status. Campus life beckoned, and he was eager to meet it, after curfew, which is when he tried to sneak out. He later explained that a Nebraska varsity basketball player, Stu Lantz, had set him up on a date.

But Dillard's teammates took the matter—him—into their own hands, without informing Marquiss. They tackled and pinned him, and refused to let him leave.

"I was one of three people holding on to Dwaine's ankle," Harvey Josin recalled. "He wanted to go down a fire escape."

Dillard stayed in and it was a good thing, too. Friday morning Marquiss told the team that he would play against Boy Town. Once again, a full police contingent—none wearing helmets this time—was on hand at Pershing Auditorium. A scattering of jeers greeted Dillard when he was announced among the starters, but there was no disturbance among the crowd of 2,450, which included several hundred more Central fans than the day before, Biddle's father among them.

As the game got underway, what they saw was unsettling. Something was out of kilter. Even with Dillard on the floor, and perhaps because of him, the Rhythm Boys could not find themselves. Boys Town controlled the tempo, and Central struggled for an answer. On the strength of Dillard's inside game Central led 27–23 at the half but fell behind 36–32 late in the third quarter. With two minutes left Hunter tied it at 41. Dillard missed a thirty-footer with three seconds left to force overtime.

In overtime Dillard put back a missed shot by Griffin for a 43–41 lead. At 43–43, Griffin took a fast-break feed from Dillard and converted a three-point play for a 46–43 lead. Griffin added another bucket, and Frazier and Dillard hit free throws to nail down the hard-fought 51–47 win.

Frazier had another solid game with twelve points. Dillard led all scorers with twenty-three points, grabbed twenty-one rebounds, and blocked four shots. Caruthers came off the bench for a short stint; otherwise, the starters played the entire game, and were spent.

Afterward, Marquiss told reporters he was "satisfied" with Dillard's performance, but wondered whether Dillard had been less aggressive than usual. Then he said something ominous. Marquiss referred back to the first-round victory over North Platte, and said, "I think emotionally we went to the peak yesterday."

Paul LeBar took Marquiss's cue and described Central as "emotionally spent, tense and severely challenged."

Central's game was without incident. Such was not the case in the other semifinal game, between Omaha Tech and Lincoln Northeast, played at another venue, the University of Nebraska Coliseum, surrounded by police. Tech was without sophomore Calvin Brown, who had been arrested with Dillard, and not allowed to suit up. The match-up, between Tech's all-black starting five and Northeast's all-white starting five, was tense and physical.

Though favored, Tech was beaten, 85–64, as Northeast hit fourteen of its first seventeen shots. But the outcome was secondary to an incident that involved Tech's leading scorer, Ernie Britt, and a white referee. With less than three minutes left, Britt was whistled for his fifth foul by referee Harland Sutton, of Chappell, in southwest Nebraska. It was a bad call, and Britt swore at Sutton. He was told to leave the court or incur a technical foul, but Britt unleashed more obscenities and Sutton called the technical.

As Sutton approached the scorer's desk at midcourt, Britt, a muscular six foot one, and two hundred pounds, came up from behind and pushed him. Sutton flew over the desk into the second row of bleachers.

"Then Britt went nuts," recalled Lyle Hiatt, a Northeast player.

He thrashed about, fists clenched, at nobody and everybody, until Bob Devaney, Nebraska's head football coach, came out of the stands and enveloped him in a bear hug. Tech fans rained snow cones, ice, and paper cups on the court, as Devaney subdued Britt and led him to the locker room. Police, with clubs drawn and dogs at their sides, ringed the court, and the final two minutes and forty-nine seconds of the game was delayed for five minutes.

"I was frustrated," Britt recalled. "I pushed the referee because I didn't commit the fifth foul."

After the game, Northeast fans remained seated until Tech fans had left the building. Outside, police broke up fights between Tech fans and white college students on their way to class.

The Britt incident thickened the pall over the tournament and gave Central's players another reason to worry. Black players from Omaha felt white officials from outside of Omaha targeted them with quick whistles, Britt recalled. Britt's phantom fifth foul, and two marginal calls early in the game, reinforced the perception.

"It was hard for us to win in Lincoln," Britt recalled.

On Friday evening the Central squad stayed in the dorm and tried to relax. A few played a card game called "tonk," Griffin among them. As the game progressed, Griffin lit up a cigarette. While Griffin smoked Marquiss came into the room on a routine check. Cigarettes were against Marquiss's rules—despite his own habit—and Griffin was about to be caught red-handed. In a flash, Griffin jammed his hand, and the cigarette, into his pants pocket.

"Marquiss talked to us, and all the while the cigarette was burning in Griffin's pocket," recalled Josin.

After what seemed like an eternity but was probably two minutes, Marquiss exited the room. Griffin pulled out the cigarette from his pocket and threw it on the floor.

"Aaaaaaah!"

He ran to a sink and held his hand under cold water. Then he poked his finger through a hole in the pocket.

"Griffin swore a blue streak and everybody about died laughing," Josin recalled.

Nerves, anticipation, and the excitement of being away from home precluded sound sleep. After Marquiss's last bed check, the players were up and out of bed.

"Most of us had never been anywhere before," Biddle recalled. "We were running around in the halls late into the night."

Sleep was not a problem for Dollis, who wrote: "I can't believe these last two days have been school days. I got to drive to Lincoln today but Mom changed her mind about letting me stay overnight with the car. Now I'm glad I didn't though because I got the flu today and I was so sick I couldn't cheer. I drove right home and went to bed. I'm still really sick but I'm going to the game anyway tomorrow."

Meanwhile, Marquiss worried about Lincoln Northeast, dubbed the "Cinderella" team by the media. Northeast was a mostly white high school located in a mostly white neighborhood affluent enough that each of the seven seniors and a couple of juniors on the team had his own car. The team had one black player, junior Harold Hill, who lived at Whitehall, a smaller version of Boys Town.

Northeast head coach Ed Johnson, like Marquiss, was in his nineteenth season, and had thinning gray hair. But unlike Marquiss, he had three championships, from 1950, 1962, and 1967, the latter at Marquiss's expense. He had lost all of his starters from the '67 team, and modest expectations for this season were fulfilled when Northeast lost six of its first ten games.

But Johnson nurtured his young squad, whose starters included two sophomores, Maury Damkroger and Tom Novak. Junior Dan Cook and seniors Lyle Hiatt and Bill Slaughter filled out the starting five, while senior Bob Jones spelled Slaughter at center. It took awhile for Johnson's system to take hold. Players were required to write a list of their on-court mistakes and discuss them in individual meetings with Johnson. If their play was subpar, they had to sit next to Johnson on the bench and listen to him teach.

His system included a methodical walk-it-up offense, set plays for situations, and rigorous conditioning. Johnson scouted opponents and constructed detailed game plans.

"You knew who was left-handed and who favored this shot or that," Hiatt recalled.

At the end of the season Northeast reeled off ten straight victories to reach the state final. It caught a break when the tournament shifted from Omaha to Lincoln, where it had home cooking, and the advantage of a home crowd. It caught another break when its first two games were played at the university Coliseum, site of the final, while Central's first two games were at Pershing Auditorium.

Central had won nineteen straight and was the tournament's top seed. Northeast had nobody of Dillard's caliber;

conventional wisdom made Central a comfortable favorite. But Central's fans were wary, as Dollis wrote, "Today we play Lincoln Northeast for the final game. We lost state to them last year. I don't want to cry again."

Saturday—Dillard's nineteenth birthday—broke mild, dry, and partly cloudy, with the temperature headed toward 55. About seven thousand fans wedged into the Coliseum, built in 1926, and known for dim lighting, loud acoustics, and cramped confines.

"The officials allowed us to have one foot in and one foot out when inbounding—that's how close the crowd was," Hunter recalled.

More than a few fans yawned before the 9:30 a.m. tip-off. Radio and TV crews from Omaha and Lincoln stations were at courtside. As in prior games, police ringed the court and took up positions in the stands and outside the building. They would have little to do on this morning except watch. Except for a few boos at Dillard's introduction, the crowd drew minimal attention to itself.

Dillard jumped against Slaughter, and thus began a game for which no film, audio, or print play-by-play survived. It is a game reconstructed through the memories of those who played and attended, and through the coverage of the Omaha and Lincoln newspapers.

It was, from the start, terribly wrong for Central, bereft of creative energy.

Defense ruled a slow first half in which both clubs carefully probed for close-in shots. In its defensive end, Northeast started in a seldom-used zone that collapsed on Dillard. When it switched to a man-to-man defense, the six-foot-five, two-

No rhythm in the final game. *From left*: Phil Griffin, Jim Martin, Warren Marquiss, John Biddle, Dwaine Dillard, and (*bent over*) Willie Frazier. Reprinted with permission of the *Omaha World-Herald*.

hundred-pound Slaughter leaned on him and drew help from his teammates. The ever-astute Johnson had assigned Hiatt to run in front of Dillard as he transitioned from defense to offense, to slow him down.

"I don't know how Coach (Johnson) came up with that, but we worked on it beforehand," Hiatt recalled.

Dillard had little room to maneuver, and committed two fouls in the first five and a half minutes. Both calls were marginal and served to arouse Central's worst fears about the officials, Dennis Logan and Dan Newmyer, both white and both from North Platte.

"I remember Dwaine looking at people like 'What did I do?'" Hunter recalled.

"The refs definitely had us targeted," Dillard recalled.

The two fouls made Dillard tentative and put the offense out of sync. Two wide-open lay-ups were missed. Only Griffin's hot hand—six baskets, most on baseline jumpers—salvaged the first half. In one stretch Griffin took Biddle's feeds and converted on four straight buckets.

Central led at halftime, 19–18, on just three points from Dillard.

"I don't know what his thought process was—he wasn't his regular self," Biddle recalled.

"Just coming out of jail, I still had charges on me with the Molotovs, and there was a lot of stress," Dillard recalled.

Both offenses tried to open up in the third quarter, and Northeast succeeded. Sophomore guard Tom Novak, whose father had been a postwar football star for Nebraska, hit three straight baskets from long range to give Northeast a 26–23 lead. When Central's zone spread out to stop Novak, the ball went inside to Damkroger and he was fouled. After Damkroger made one free throw, Novak stole the inbounds pass and converted for another basket. On Northeast's next possession he potted · his fifth basket of the quarter.

"Coach wanted us to play a confined zone to protect the middle—they had Damkroger penetrating," Hunter recalled. "We closed it up and they hit from way outside. A couple of times we went out and confronted them, but maybe we should have done more."

Northeast moved out to a 35–27 lead with a minute and forty-five seconds left in the third quarter. Central's offense continued to sputter, as its one hot shooter, Griffin, found the ball hard to come by.

"They should have directed more stuff to me in the second half," Griffin recalled.

"Maybe I should have stayed with him longer," Biddle recalled. "But as the point guard I had to spread it—I couldn't let one guy do it."

Late in the third quarter, Dillard finally got untracked. It helped that Northeast's Hiatt, who had dogged his footsteps in transition, fouled out. A couple of baskets by Dillard cut Northeast's lead to 36–34 after three quarters. Midway through the fourth quarter, Northeast widened its lead to 46–40 on baskets by Cook and Slaughter.

With a little more than three minutes left Central applied a full-court press. Effective throughout the season, the press now produced nothing, as Northeast beat it with disciplined ball movement, and drew a couple of fouls to boot.

In the final two minutes both Dillard and Biddle were whistled for offensive fouls—marginal calls that could have gone the other way—which deprived Central of possession and sent Northeast to the line. Twice, Cook hit both ends of a one-and-one, and Novak made two free throws.

Lincoln Northeast 54, Omaha Central 50.

Upset.

Final statistics: Northeast hit 59 percent from the field in the second half, and twelve of fifteen from the line. Novak's sixteen led Northeast, while Slaughter added eleven. Central hit 37.7 percent from the field and ten of twenty from the line. Dillard led all scorers with twenty-two points, on eight-for-seventeen shooting, and seventeen rebounds, of which six were offensive, all in the second half. Griffin added thirteen first-half points. Hunter had six, Frazier five, and Biddle four.

Bedlam in the Northeast stands contrasted with silent gloom on the Central side. Hunter was photographed in tears, as was cheerleader Frankie Weiner.

The trophy presentation followed. The players shook hands, and Central stood off to the side as Johnson and his squad hoisted the hardware. As trophy presentations go, it was typical—exciting and banal. But it was a moment Hiatt remembered for a special reason.

"Tech had been incredibly unsportsmanlike and we had expected the same from Central," Hiatt recalled. "But they played completely the way high school sports should be played. When they lost they were disappointed but not angry, and you didn't hear a bad word. They were good sports when they shook hands. You came away thinking 'I wouldn't mind going to Central.' It seemed like a cool school."

The Coliseum emptied without incident, as both coaches talked to media. Johnson expressed relief that the players and fans had behaved well. He complimented Slaughter's defensive effort against Dillard, and credited Novak and Damkroger for their unsophomorelike play.

When asked if Northeast's victory meant it was the better team, Johnson paused.

"It means we were better today," he replied. "But it just means today, and of course, tomorrow doesn't count anymore."

The crestfallen Marquiss put up a brave front, "his head as high as ever," it was reported. Marquiss echoed Johnson in lauding the behavior of the players and fans. His team lost because it shot poorly, and not because of the opponent's defense, he said. The defensive effort was adequate, he said. What beat Central, he suggested, was an emotional nadir.

"We were emotionally drained, I guess we were flat," he said.

It would have helped, he went on, if Central had played a game, or been allowed to practice on the Coliseum floor before the final, but such were "the breaks."

"I'd like also to have had a week with less emotion and tension, but that's life, too," he added.

That was it. A high school basketball championship had been decided. Some people looked at it as nothing more and moved on. Others could not help but see more.

Columnist Hal Brown, in the *Lincoln Sunday Journal and Star*, wrote:

We have in this country cities covering several square miles where the two races cannot get along even under noncompetitive conditions. Yet five Negroes from Omaha Central and five Whites from Lincoln Northeast proved Saturday morning that the two races can get along even in an area only 94 by 50 feet.

Brown added a sentence that was naïve, or racist, or both:

If the Omaha Negroes responsible for the Monday night troubles in their city had been able to show the restraint under stress that was shown by the Central Negro cagers, the Class A competition would have been played in Omaha Saturday night instead of in Lincoln Saturday morning.

The Sunday newspaper reported that "the student body of Omaha Central—denied its first state basketball championship since 1912 by a band of Lincoln Northeast miracle workers—stood tall in its agony Saturday."

The article quoted a Lincoln cop, Gordon Cox, who had been at courtside: "I'll say one thing for Central, they're the best in the world in sportsmanship."

Not everybody was satisfied. A *World-Herald* reader, Mrs. Richard R. Keely, in a public letter, criticized school officials for allowing Dillard to play, and said they should "hang their head in shame."

"With apparently intelligent persons making such decisions how do we teach our youth to respect anything or any one?" Keely wrote.

Sarcasm crept into the commentary of *Register* sports editor Gary Soiref, who wrote: "It is true that Central played one of its poorer games of the season against Northeast, something that usually happens to them around the time of the state finals."

Soiref went on: "I believe sincerely that this year's team was one of the most talented high school ball clubs from this area in at least a decade. . . . Northeast outplayed us that one day but by no means, in my opinion, were they of the same caliber as The Rhythm Boys."

Further analysis, if it occurred, was beneath the sports media radar, not yet the carpet-bomb model of the twenty-first century. If the game had been a referendum on the ability of the two races to get along, was it not also a referendum on two basketball philosophies, between Northeast's structure and Central's improvisation?

Johnson had looked like an orchestra conductor as he directed his young team. Marquiss had sat back and let his team run itself, as it had for most of the season. When Northeast's guards heated up from outside in the third quarter, Central's response was slow. When Biddle decided to spread the offense instead of going to his hot shooter, Griffin, the decision was his alone.

And if it was a referendum on two philosophies, was it not, by extension, a microcosm of the sixties?

Deep stuff. Then again, maybe it was no deeper than the foul line: Northeast twelve for fifteen, Central ten for twenty.

"It came down to free-throw shooting," Hiatt recalled. "Quite frankly, I don't know how we won. If we had played ten times that's probably the one time we would have won."

Hunter agreed that free throws were pivotal, but said the contest should never have been that close. It was, he said, because he and his teammates "never found our rhythm." They had endured the Wallace rally, their neighborhood aflame, Dillard's arrest, the unexpected road trip, the game without Dillard, and the grinder over Boys Town. By the time they reached the final, he said, they were "emotionally spent."

Dollis told what became of the broken hearted in her diary entry for Sunday, March 10:

I was really sick all day today. I didn't go to church because my stomach hurt so bad. But I wasn't the only one feeling bad. Willie's brother, Ernie, (he's 22 and Willie lives with him and his wife, Celestine) called me this afternoon and said he was really worried because Willie was so depressed. He wanted me to come over to see him and try to cheer him up, but I was too sick. So I called Willie later and tried to talk, but he feels bad about losing yesterday and he's really discouraged.

So ended a week of passion, adrenaline, anger, fear, and sorrow. A week to shout, fight, and embrace. A week to grow.

12

Last Bell

Everything and nothing was the same. People climbed out of bed, brushed their teeth, gulped cereal, and got off to Central. Cars were parked, coats were hung, books were opened. Life resumed. Sort of.

Roy Hunter rode the bus from Thirty-third and Ames, and noticed something different.

"People were really quiet," Hunter recalled. "Usually there was conversation."

At Central it was the same—quiet and too polite.

"The whole atmosphere had changed," Hunter recalled. "People were nice but we didn't have the camaraderie we had before the game."

White and black students were especially careful around one another. One biracial couple, Delmar Givehand and Diane Jacobson, called it off, at least for awhile.

"We started having a problem—the atmosphere was just weird," Givehand recalled.

Even traditional allies, blacks and Jews, found relations strained. Jawanda Gauff recalled being asked by a Jewish classmate why black protesters firebombed their own neighborhood.

"Why take out your own merchants?" he said. "Go down-town if you're angry about something."

She could not disagree.

"All of a sudden school was divided," Gauff recalled. "I had never felt that in my three years at Central."

The distance between friends was painful to some. Howie Halperin's buddy, Vince Orduna, ignored him as they passed in the hall.

"We had had a pretty good relationship—now he didn't want anything to do with me," Halperin recalled.

Nelson, ever crusty, pounced on those who had missed school. He urged teachers to administer tests—immediately—on les-sons from the prior week. "It's a device we use to get their minds back to business right away and show them how far behind they are in their work," Nelson told the *World-Herald*.

Within a week the *Register* bannered an editorial atop page one: "Recent Disturbances Affect Central Students."

The disturbances, it concluded, showed

that the Hilltop, usually the epitome of racial harmony, may be disrupted by senselessness. It shows that students in school, often heralded nationally as topnotch, may suffer for the wrongs of a few—both white and black. The reputation of Central has been bruised but not permanently. . . . The outlook is optimistic—for this Omaha and Central may be proud. But the grim facts of the week of March 4 remain. Friends, good friends, saw how ugly it is to hate each other because of skin color.

On March 20, two weeks after Dillard's release from jail, the county attorney dropped his charges, due to insufficient evidence. The media, which had milked the story, now provided no reaction from Dillard, Marquiss, Nelson, Chambers, or police.

Charges also were dropped against Calvin Webster, Calvin Brown, Lloyd Brown, and David Russ. The driver, Nathaniel Goodwin, was bound over for trial, charged with possessing an explosive and carrying a concealed weapon. The off-duty cop, James Abbott, who killed Howard Stevenson, was not charged because the shooting was said to have occurred during a burglary attempt.

The next evening Central's Road Show started. In what was believed to be a first for the annual variety show, it featured an all-black group, The Soul Serenaders, whose members included Phil Allison, a basketball reserve. Lead singer Shirley Bailey delivered "Oh How it Hurts," a plaintive R&B number. The lyrics, "Oh how it hurts / to say good-bye / Oh how it hurts / For me to cry," found their mark in the bruised collective psyche. A standing ovation rocked the old theater-auditorium, in a glimpse of *Fame* and *Glee*.

Before the month was out Dillard visited Eastern Michigan University, in Ypsilanti, Michigan, on his first recruiting trip. Up until his arrest, several major colleges had contacted him, including Davidson, Duke, UCLA, Kansas, and Lafayette. Langston, an all-black college in Oklahoma, had expressed interest not only in Dillard but the other four starters as well. After his arrest the calls dried up, and Dillard was grateful for the offer from Eastern Michigan. His visit to the Ypsilanti campus included a couple of dates with college girls.

"That played a big part in my decision," Dillard recalled.

When streams were ripe and swelled with rain, April came, and Dillard left. He was expelled from Central for behavior deemed intolerable now that basketball was over. The incident that triggered his expulsion has been lost in time, but it wasn't the first. In another incident he and two or three teammates were disciplined for stealing items from a locker at Norris Junior High. His suspension for use of "foul language," his incineration of a trashcan the day after the Wallace event, and his hamburger-bun attack on a teacher all added to his dossier.

Dillard's "Personality Record," kept by his guidance counselor, suggested that the front office was not fond of him. On a scale of one to five, with one being the best and five the worst, Dillard scored a five on responsibility and adjustability. He scored a four on initiative, work habits, and cooperation, and a three on personal appearance.

His attendance record showed that of one hundred and thirty school days, he had been absent for twenty-one and a half and tardy for nine.

Dillard's classroom work was not strong enough to overcome his other problems. His first semester grades, with one being the highest and five a failing grade, were fives in Bookkeeping and General Shop, a four in Refresher Math, and threes in Art and Music. His biggest problem was reading—on a standard reading test he placed in the lowest 10 percent of aptitude.

One of Dillard's courses second semester was General English, taught by Tim Schmad. In five previous semesters of General English Dillard had earned four fours and one five.

"He wasn't motivated," Schmad recalled. "He had the notion that he didn't need to study because he would be a basketball player his whole life."

That Central saw fit to live with Dillard's behavior, absentee-ism, and poor grades through the basketball season, but not after, reinforced the views advanced by Harry Edwards and Steve Moss. In their view, Dillard had been used, and Central had not acted in his best interest.

Early in April Dillard cleaned out his locker. His departure deprived his classmates of his upbeat, outsized personality, and left a melancholy void in the old wooden hallways.

Another classmate followed Dillard out the door. Sue Glyn dropped out, at her parents' insistence, after she told them of her pregnancy. She checked into a home for unwed mothers and waited to give birth. No visitors came, not even the unborn child's father, Frazier.

Once, at a grocery store, where she had gone to buy candy, Glyn ran into her father, whom she had not seen in weeks. She said hello, and watched heartbroken as he glared and walked away.

"I was a pariah." Glyn recalled. "At that time it was the most shameful, heinous thing a girl could do."

High school life competed with an onrush of national events. In the first presidential primary, March 12 in New Hampshire, an antiwar candidate, Democratic senator Eugene McCarthy tallied 42 percent against President Johnson. Encouraged by McCarthy's showing, Democratic senator Robert Kennedy jumped into the race, and set up a Nebraska headquarters at the Sheraton Fontenelle Hotel, about four blocks from Central. Late in March Johnson withdrew from the race, which al-tered Wallace's political calculus, and ensured an even wilder scramble for the Democratic nomination. Soon enough, Vice President Hubert H. Humphrey jumped in.

On April 4, a white assassin—a former Wallace campaign worker—murdered Dr. Martin Luther King in Memphis. At Central, teachers sat at the front of classrooms with hands folded and heads bowed, unable to speak, and students wept. King's death reminded Steve Moss of the assassination of President John F. Kennedy.

"It had the same effect on me," Moss recalled. "It put a hole in your stomach."

Numerous inner cities went up in flames, but the Near North Side was quiet, spent from the Wallace ordeal. Wallace used the civil disorder to his political advantage, but then Wallace's campaign went quiet when his wife Lurleen, the governor of Alabama, came home from the hospital to die from cancer.

Harry Edwards designated his planned Olympic boycott as "a solemn memorial to Dr. King and his family." Later in April, faced with the threat of a mass defection by forty nations, the International Olympic Committee banned South Africa from the '68 Summer Games. Soon, Edwards downgraded the boycott to a protest, in which black athletes would compete, but were to demonstrate against racism.

As the school year winded down, the Rhythm Boys planned their immediate future. Hunter took a scholarship to play at the junior college in North Platte, the small town that had lost to Central in the tournament. Biddle signed on with Dana College in Blair, Nebraska. Griffin opted for work rather than college, and had to attend summer school to graduate, due to a failing grade in American History. Frazier, short of graduation credits, decided to attend Tech for the fall semester.

Dillard enrolled in Omaha's School of Continuing Education to get his general equivalency diploma. On a Saturday evening, in late April, he showed up on Fairacres Road, at the edge of Bagel, for a party at the sumptuous home of Paul Oostenbrug and his sister Nancy Oostenbrug. The unexpectedly large gathering, remembered by Nancy as "a bit of a mob scene," included both Central and Tech basketball players, Ernie Britt among them. Partygoers drank and gambled in the basement, to the dismay of the Oostenbrugs' father, Bill.

At the back of the Oostenbrugs' long driveway, on a rickety hoop, Dillard and Ernie Britt, old adversaries, were locked in a one-on-one contest. The two had butted heads on playground courts, at the Bryant Center, and in high school games, and were rivals. Their match started at half-speed, but quickly escalated. A crowd gathered to watch them push, collide, and slam-dunk with force.

Jack Slosburg, who lived near the Oostenbrugs, worried that they were on the verge of a brawl, and had a word with Dillard. When play resumed, Britt barreled into Dillard, who wrapped him in a bear hug, and said, "Okay, it's over." Britt shrugged, Dillard threw an arm around his shoulder, and they walked off the court.

"Dwaine was a calming influence," Nancy Oostenbrug recalled.

When the party broke up one of the black attendees thanked her and promised, in jest, that "when the riots come" her house would be spared.

On May 14 Kennedy won the Nebraska primary with 51 percent to McCarthy's 31 percent, and carried 85 percent of the black vote. Richard Nixon won on the Republican side, with 71 percent to 22 percent for the runner-up, California governor Ronald Reagan. Out of 345,000 votes cast, Wallace polled just 2,500, split amongst his third party and write-ins on the Democratic and Republican ballots.

J. Arthur Nelson Day, an event to honor the outgoing principal, was held at Central on Sunday May 19. The school color guard presented the flag, the A Cappella Choir sang four songs, and testimonial speeches were given by, among others, Dr. G. T. Monsoon, the pastor of Augustana Lutheran Church, and state senator Edward W. Danner, who represented the Near North Side. The assistant principal, Moller, was poised to succeed Nelson.

The '68 Central yearbook, known as the *O-Book*, came out. Atop page 85, above individual photos of Dillard (whose first name was misspelled as "Dwain"), Frazier, Biddle, Griffin, and Hunter, was the lowercase title, "the rhythm boys." *O-Book* sports editor Andy Liberman had overcome the reluctance of journalism instructor Mike Gaherty to get it in print.

"Maybe he thought the phrase had sexual or racial connotations — that was the kind of reaction he had," Liberman recalled. "I just thought it was our name for the team, and it was cool."

The shock of King's murder was replicated, almost beyond belief, on June 6, as a Palestinian immigrant gunned down Kennedy after he won the California primary. Once again, teachers and students were stricken with grief, among them Darryl Eure, who had volunteered for Kennedy, and who clung to a photo of the candidate shaking his hand as he campaigned, in a downpour, on the Near North Side.

Dollis wrote in her June 8 entry:

I woke up at 8 and I almost had the feeling Robert Kennedy had died even before I found out. I spent the night with Diane and she took me home early. Every time I heard the news today I cried. I went up to Field Club at 12:30 and by 3 I was so sunburned I came home. It's funny how life goes on and people are only partially touched by tragedy. Violence is becoming accepted as a part of life even though we try to think we just can't ever learn to tolerate it. I don't really tolerate it, but like everyone else, I am forced to live with it. My own reaction to things that are happening in this country is disappointment and I am saddened into believing there's nothing I can do about it.

The class of 1968 was graduated on Saturday, June 8, at the Civic Auditorium Arena, where three months earlier Wallace had incited a riot. Bob Guss, whose punishment for lunchhour merriment as a sophomore had been to eat in the "black" cafeteria, and who was headed to Yale, gave the senior oration, but only after it was cleansed of political dissent by Moller.

"Mind you, he did it politely," recalled Guss. "He attached a cartoon to a final draft that had a mounted knight in armor telling his attendant, 'Point me towards the establishment!'"

Biddle, Hunter, Griffin, and Moss were listed in the commencement booklet, Griffin and Moss as August graduates. Dillard and Frazier were not listed.

After his March 4 appearance, Wallace had not set foot in Nebraska. His campaign's announcement, in midsummer, that he would return in September, was met with resistance. One letter, to "Concerned Citizens of Omaha," urged that security be provided "to prevent the Wallace staff and his hired security guards from using and exploiting any demonstrators present," and suggested that Governor Norbert Tiemann "advise Mr. Wallace accordingly" if "proper safeguards cannot be assured." Five women activists, Diana Hahn, Susie (Thompson)

Buffett (Central class of 1950), Shirley Lipsey (Central class of 1944), Denyse Adler, and Evelyn Zysman (Central class of 1927), signed the letter.

Early in August, Glyn gave birth to a boy. Frazier visited her at the hospital and they settled on a name, Robert Charles, the latter being Frazier's middle name. Adoption plans had been made, but Frazier asked her to keep the baby and she agreed.

Absent support from her family or Frazier, Glyn lived with Frazier's sister and her five children in the projects, and took a job as a nurse's aid, on the evening shift. Ten days into the job, while at work, she was stricken with a complication from her pregnancy, lost a large amount of blood, and was taken to the emergency room.

Now Glyn's coworkers knew that she was an unwed mother, and she was too ashamed to return to work.

"I was alone, penniless, and defeated," Glyn recalled.

She called her parents, who agreed to let her return home, but only if she put her "bastard child" up for adoption. She conceded.

"It was the most gut-wrenching of emotions to hand over my baby," Glyn recalled. "I know I will never again feel that much pain. Nothing compares."

The Rhythm Boys, minus Hunter, had a last hurrah, late in August, at the high school All-Star Game at the Civic Auditorium. Dillard, Frazier, Biddle, and Griffin played together for much of the game, on the losing National team. Foul trouble slowed Dillard, but Frazier led the Nationals with nineteen, followed by Griffin with thirteen, and Biddle with ten.

Marquiss, now retired as a coach but still wounded, gave an interview to the new *Register* sports editor—me—in September, in which he said, "The fairest way to hold a state tournament would be to have a double-elimination tournament."

Vikki Dollis, now a senior in the new school year, was nominated for homecoming queen and wrote on September 27:

Today was a strange day . . . Frankie and Betsy and I went out to breakfast before school which is something different. Then after school Mike Paladino, a boy I used to like when I was a sophomore, asked me out for tomorrow night. I was really surprised. Then after the game all of us girls were in Bagel and I asked Steve Marantz to be my escort for Homecoming and he asked me to be his date! I'm so excited because he's so nice! I talked to Ernie Frazier tonite and he says Willie really loves me. I saw him (Willie) at the game tonite and I still like him.

Dillard was at Eastern Michigan that fall when the Revolt of the Black Athlete enjoyed two climactic moments. On October 6, University of Nebraska at Omaha's Marlin Briscoe, a rookie with the Denver Broncos, became the first black to start at quarterback in the modern NFL era. Before the season was out, Briscoe started seven games and played in four others, threw fourteen touchdown passes, and shattered the stereotype of black quarterbacks.

In mid-October, in the Summer Olympics at Mexico City, two black American sprinters, Tommie Smith and John Carlos, placed first and third in the 200-meter race. They climbed the victory stand shoeless, each wearing black socks and a single black glove. The gloves, they later explained, symbolized the power and unity of black America, and black socks with no shoes symbolized its poverty.

At the playing of the U.S. national anthem, Smith and Carlos raised their gloved fists and bowed their heads, an image of protest that shocked and inspired viewers around the world.

Dollis and Frazier parted. Derek Majors, a blonde, blue-eyed quarterback, caught the attention of Dollis, who wrote on October 17: "I hope it's Derek I'm in love with and not just love. . . . It is still a new feeling for me and I like it but I'm so afraid of my fickleness for Derek's sake."

Two nights later Dollis wrote about homecoming:

All day I worried and I was so scared about Homecoming tonite. But it was all in vain. I knew there would be times in my life when I would have to face defeat. Tonite was just the beginning. Frankie Weiner is Homecoming queen. I can't say it doesn't hurt to lose, but it is even more painful to be a good loser. . . . I should be paying more attention to my date but I'm thinking about Derek.

In the November presidential election, Wallace carried five southern states, worth forty-six electoral votes, and won almost ten million votes, about 13.5 percent. As he expected, in the North and Midwest his appeal to union members and blue-collar workers hurt the Democratic candidate, Hubert Humphrey, more than the Republican candidate, Richard Nixon. By November the fractured Democrats were less able to withstand Wallace defections than the Republicans, and Nixon won the presidency with 301 electoral votes.

Nixon's electoral vote total included five from Nebraska, where 8.3 percent of the vote went for Wallace, who never did return for a second campaign rally.

If Wallace and Humphrey had won just thirty-two more electoral votes, Nixon would have been denied an outright victory, and the House of Representatives would have decided the outcome. A change of 41,971 votes from Nixon to Humphrey (.06 percent of the national total) in three states (Missouri 10,245, New Jersey 30,631, Alaska 1,095) would have resulted in no electoral majority. Not since Wallace in 1968 has a third-party presidential candidate won an electoral vote.

By the end of 1968, Nathaniel Goodwin was convicted of possession of a firebomb and a concealed weapon, and sentenced to one to three years in state prison. Goodwin appealed and lost before the Supreme Court of Nebraska.

At Eastern Michigan Dillard was the lone freshman starter, but found Ypsilanti too small and confined. He left in his second year, hung out in Omaha, and then went to the Bay Area, to be near his father, in the summer of 1971. He established himself in local gyms, caught the eye of a coach, and was offered a scholarship to tiny St. Mary's College in Moraga, California. But Moraga was another small town, which Dillard found dull, and he was barely there a week before he showed up at a municipal gym in Berkeley. There, he went up against Phil Chenier, Cal-Berkeley's star guard, who was impressed.

"Dwaine was dominating," Chenier recalled. "Shooting his midrange jumper, dunking on people, running the floor. We were trying to figure out who this guy was."

Chenier told Cal's coach, Jim Padgett, that he had discovered a "Sidney Wicks type of player" — a reference to the UCLA All-American. Padgett watched Dillard play in a pick-up game and afterward, over pizza, offered Dillard a scholarship.

"That night, in my car, we go out to St. Mary's, like thieves in the night, and he gathers up all his stuff," Chenier recalled. "He doesn't tell anybody he is leaving and he sneaks out of there."

Chenier and Dillard shared an apartment as Padgett processed the paperwork for his scholarship. When Chenier went off to a tryout camp for the Pan-American Games, Dillard went to Omaha, to visit his mother. He never returned. Chenier got back to Berkeley and took a call from Dillard.

"I'm not coming back," Dillard said. "Can you send my stuff to Omaha?"

"What?"

"I need to stay with my mom."

Dillard offered no further explanation. Chenier decided to forego his senior season at Cal, convinced that without Dillard a conference title was unobtainable, and was taken in the NBA supplemental draft by the Baltimore Bullets. Chenier and Dillard lost touch, as Chenier enjoyed a solid rookie season. Baltimore took Dillard in the fifth round of the 1972 draft, and he called Chenier for advice.

"Be in the best shape of your life—the two-a-days take a toll," Chenier told him.

Dillard went to Baltimore's tryout camp and was one of the last to be cut. Chenier thought that Dillard's conditioning, after years of smoking, hurt him.

"He had the skills but he still smoked," Chenier recalled.

"It was just a numbers game, too. Unfortunately Dwaine didn't have the leverage of someone from a Division I school or someone taken in the first or second round."

Discouraged, Dillard was hired by the vaudevillian Harlem Globetrotters and assigned to their clueless foils, the Washington Generals. Eventually he was promoted to the Globetrotters. The Globetrotters put money in Dillard's pocket, which he lavished on family and friends, but cost him something, too.

Dwaine Dillard failed to make the NBA but caught on with the Harlem Globetrotters. Photo courtesy of Carlos Dillard.

Jack Olsen, in his 1968 *Sports Illustrated* series, described the Globetrotters as "the white man's favorite black road show."

"The Trotters help to perpetuate the Negro stereotype," Olsen wrote.

Running about the court emitting savage jungle yells, shouting in thick Southern accents ("Yassuh, yassuh"), pulling sly larcenous tricks like walking with the ball when the (white) referee's back is turned, calling one another inane names like Sweetwater and Showboat, they come across as frivolous, mildly dishonest children, the white man's encapsulated view of the whole Negro race set to the bouncy rhythms of their theme song, "Sweet Georgia Brown."

By 1974 the Globetrotters were even more of a racial anachronism. Dillard's dignity was bruised, even as a bitter memory ate at him. He warned a few of Central's players before the 1974 state tournament, "You'll never win down there [Lincoln] — they won't let you win." But the '74 squad proved him wrong and won Central's first state title since 1912.

Dillard quit in 1976 rather than tour with the Globetrotters' European squad. Nothing came of a tryout with the Carolina Cougars of the American Basketball Association. But the Utah Stars — encouraged by "Ironman" Ron Boone (from the Tech High School class of '64), a native Omahan and friend of Dillard — hired him for a short stint in 1976. Dillard got into three games, played nineteen minutes, and recorded four points, nine rebounds, two assists, two steals, two blocked shots, five turnovers, and seven fouls. That was the sum of his professional career, and the end of his dream. He brooded and grew bitter.

"He beat himself up a lot with coulda, woulda, shoulda," recalled Shauntoi Jackson, his younger sister. "He kicked himself over a few bad decisions he made."

Said Barbara Essex: "I think not making it to the pros really messed him up."

Out of high-level basketball, Dillard drank more. He worked a variety of jobs, including a stint as a security guard at the Douglas County Courthouse in Omaha, and had little contact with his son, Brian, born to Essex in 1973, or daughter, Jennifer Troia, born in 1981. The mother of another boy, Darnell Clark, claimed Dillard was his father, and though Dillard denied it, he did not contest her claim.

There was a brief marriage in Dallas in the mid-1980s, to Ruth Stoker, during which he met Rochelle Epps, a divorced mother of two in Oklahoma City. They became a couple, and Dillard found work as a youth councilor with the city, teaching basketball, while Rochelle worked in computers.

But in 1988 Dillard moved back to California, to be near his father, Rufus Dwaine, still a cook in the state prison system. Rochelle followed him, and in 1989 they married in Sonoma County. Again, Dillard found work with disadvantaged youth. Dwaine, Jr., was born in 1990. Dillard seemed content, until Rufus Dwaine passed away early in 1991.

"He fell apart when he lost his dad," Rochelle recalled.

Dillard went on a "six-month drinking binge," she recalled, and was physically abusive. Rochelle moved back to Oklahoma City in July 1991 and Dillard soon followed. Her work in computers supported them, and they had a daughter, Carolee, in 1994. As their children grew up, Dillard was reluctant to play basketball with them.

"He was so bitter about basketball," she recalled. "He didn't want to talk much about it. He thought he should have gone further."

Dillard moved to Phoenix in 1999 and divorced Rochelle in 2000. He found a job at a courthouse, but after 9/11 he moved back to Omaha and went to work for the new federal Transportation Security Administration, inspecting baggage at Eppley Airfield. Then he transferred to a similar position at Sky Harbor Airport in Phoenix. Dillard spent time with his siblings, manned a backyard grill with distinction, and became something of a beloved uncle to his nieces and nephews. His drinking continued. "Black Velvet—his 'cup of tea' as he called it," recalled Shauntoi. "By day he was sweet and nice, but you had to step back when he started drinking his special tea."

Dillard's health declined early in 2007. His stomach bloated and his bowels locked up, but he put off seeing a doctor. At the insistence of his siblings, he went in for an exam and was diagnosed with pancreatic cancer. He underwent surgery in October 2007 and was advised to undergo chemotherapy, but declined.

"He kept saying he didn't need chemo," Rochelle recalled.

By the spring of 2008 his weight had dropped from 250 to 125, even as he insisted he was not sick. Rochelle drove Dwaine Jr. and Carolee out from Oklahoma City to be with him. She drove back, but they stayed, and were there when he died on June 25, 2008, at the age of fifty-nine.

His funeral in Phoenix was attended by two Central friends, John Biddle and Dr. Khalid Kamal, the former Lindbergh White. After the service Kamal told one of Dillard's sisters, "I looked up to Dwaine." Biddle stood among Dillard's children, nieces, and nephews, choked back a tear, and began:

"We had a team. They called us the Rhythm Boys."

13

Their Beat Goes On

In 2008, the year Dillard died, Ernie Chambers retired from the Nebraska legislature, and Barack Obama was elected president. The three events were connected by a distant and wistful karma.

Chambers had arranged Dillard's release without bail the morning of March 6, 1968. In 1970 Chambers was elected from the Near North Side and served as Nebraska's only African American state senator for thirty-eight years until a term-limits law forced him out. In office, Chambers—a political independent and contrarian—was a forceful, articulate, and occasionally spiteful advocate for the rights of African Americans.

Dillard's rights, under siege from Wallace, were the issues that put him in the national news. Obama was six years old when Wallace came to Omaha. Wallace's politics of race and class were the antithesis of Obama's, forty years later, but they were the politics that threatened Dillard, and likely led him to Nate Goodwin's car that fateful night.

Go back to the evening of March 5, 1968. Dillard and his buddy, Calvin Webster, were at the outdoor courts of the Bryant Center on Twenty-fourth Street. Among others at the center were Ernie Britt, Johnny Rodgers, Jonathon Ray, and James

Glass, four Tech students. Britt, Rodgers, and Ray were start-ers on Tech's team, one of the eight, along with Central, that had advanced to the Class A State Tournament scheduled two days hence. Glass was their friend, as well as Dillard's and Webster's.

At about 11:00 p.m., closing time at the center, a disturbance broke out about a block away, at a vacant lot next to the E-Z Drive package liquor store.

"The cops started hassling somebody—there was fighting," Glass recalled.

Those at the Bryant Center moved toward the disturbance. Some proceeded with caution, others tossed rocks at the police cars. Halfway down the block, Britt, Rodgers, Ray, and Glass made a decision.

"Ernie went on home," Glass recalled. "Johnny Rodgers and Johnny Ray went home. They knew state was coming up. I left, too."

Dillard and Webster continued toward the melee. A few minutes later Goodwin pulled up in his car, and Dillard and Webster piled in, along with Calvin Brown, Lloyd Brown, and David Russ. The rest is mystery.

Why did Dillard put himself at risk? Why did he ride in a car of six young African American males on a night thick with tension and a neighborhood dense with police?

The term "racial profiling"—targeting for suspicion of crime based on race, ethnicity, religion, or national origin—had not been coined in 1968, but it was a fact of life for young black males.

"If you were riding six deep in a car you were going to get stopped, absolutely," Glass recalled.

"Dwaine was socially advanced," recalled Delmar Givehand. "He knew he put himself in a position to be arrested."

Upon his release, Dillard told his coach, Warren Marquiss, that he had been an innocent victim. He told his mother something quite different, which led her to believe he was out to "crucify" Wallace.

Early in June 2008, I spoke with Dillard by telephone. In our hour-long conversation he mentioned that he had recently come out of the hospital, but did not elaborate, His voice was clear, and his mood upbeat. Eventually the interview swung toward his arrest.

"What happened that night?"

"I wish I knew."

"What were you thinking?"

"I was eighteen. Maybe nothing. Maybe a lot of things. I was stirred up."

He offered no more, and I filed it away for future discussion. His answer can be taken one of two ways. Either he blundered into the situation, or he waded in of his own volition. If the latter, he made a risky choice, though to what extent he may not have known. If he indeed was unaware of the firebombs, he knew that racial profiling was routine.

He was innocent of a crime, as prosecutors affirmed two weeks later when his charges were dropped. But Dillard had walked a fine line as a provocateur. He did so as film audiences were mesmerized by the outlaw protagonists of *Bonnie and Clyde*, of whom director Arthur Penn had said, "[T]hey became folk heroes, violators of the status quo. And in that context, one finds oneself . . . confronted with the terrible irony that we root for somebody . . . who, in the course of a good cause, is called upon to commit acts of violence which repel us."

Dillard became a "Symbol," as columnist Wally Provost wrote. To some he was "all that they feared from lawlessness." To others he was an "idolized rebel."

He had reason to revolt. Bonnie and Clyde's saga played out, Penn had said, "at a time when very rural people were suffering the terrors of a depression." Dillard's arrest occurred as his neighborhood was at an economic precipice, and its dignity and future challenged by the "nutcase," as Nebraska's Governor Norbert Tiemann described Wallace. His childhood phantoms of abandonment and dislocation rode shotgun that night, as did perhaps a latent cynicism about a high school that feted him for basketball as he struggled to read and write. There was anger in Dillard, a streak of social outrage, a bit of Ernie Chambers.

"Ernie turned me on to the black power movement," Dillard recalled.

But what if Dillard, indeed, had blundered into trouble? Even if that were the case, the public never thought so. Millions of Americans who watched the news on March 6 knew only that Nebraska's best high school basketball player, an eighteen-year-old African American, was charged with possession of firebombs. To those viewers, Dillard's arrest put a face on the riot incited by Wallace—and raised a blinking yellow caution light above his candidacy.

At worst, Dillard was an outlaw rebel, and at best, a noble one. If he stumbled into trouble by accident he was an unintentional rebel. If he was unaware of the firebombs, but knew he might be racially profiled, he was Rosa Parks. If he understood that his athletic celebrity would magnify his protest, he was Tommie Smith and John Carlos before Tommie Smith and John Carlos.

Dillard died two and a half weeks after we talked, to my sorrow and regret. A little more than four months after Dillard's death, Obama took one electoral vote out of Nebraska, from the 2nd Congressional District, which includes Omaha. If winners write history, I like to think that, in the end, the Rhythm Boys were winners, too.

But Dillard's legacy is more timeless and universal than even politics. If Vikki Dollis's diaries reveal anything, it is need in the heart of a teenager. I remember the ache. Like all of us, Dillard searched for love and acceptance. That he did so on a public stage only increased his need. Dillard should be remembered for the fragility and courage of youth, and with the love and acceptance he craved.

If we could speak again, through the ether, I imagine this exchange:

"Do you realize what you accomplished?" I would ask.

"What?"

"You were part of a movement that changed America."

"Changed how?"

"We have an African American president."

"No."

"Yes. And you had a hand in it. If George Wallace had succeeded no telling where we'd be."

There would be a pause.

"Thank you."

"Another thing," I would say.

"Yes?"

"The Rhythm Boys were the best damn high school basketball team I ever saw. I'll never forget you."

"It was a long time ago."

"I see you clear as yesterday, running the floor, with hoop dreams and all of life ahead. Forever young."

"Eternal youth?" he would say.

"Yes."

There would be a pause.

"That works both ways, you know. If we get eternal youth, our fans get the same deal."

"All of your fans—forever young?"

"Yes."

"Right on."

"Cool."

Black palm on white, hereafter to here, skin would be given and received.

Postscript

Phil Griffin married soon out of high school, became a father in 1969, and worked at a packinghouse. He played basketball at Grandview Junior College and the University of Nebraska at Omaha, but left school in 1971 when his second son was born. Throughout the 1970s, now the father of three sons, he worked for the U.S. Post Office, United Parcel Service, and eventually the Happy Cab Company. Griffin divorced in 1979, remarried a year later, and stayed with Happy Cab, as a driver and dispatcher, until 1990, when he became a long-haul truck driver, based in Omaha. His three sons, Philip Jr., Donnell, and Carl were Central graduates, and Philip Jr. played basketball under Jim Martin, his father's junior varsity coach in 1967. Carl's twin daughters, Carnetta and Carletta, are in the Central High class of 2011. Carnetta is a cheerleader, and Carletta is the third generation of Griffins to play basketball for Central.

In his eighteen-wheeler, Griffin is on the road eleven hours a day, three hundred days a year, and hauls fruit, vegetables, meat, and wine, among other products. Most of his runs are to the West Coast, and some to Arizona and Texas.

"Technology takes away a lot of jobs, but somebody still has to drive the truck—they're never going to send the truck down the road electronically," Griffin said.

"I guess I'll keep doing it until I'm sick of it. I know guys in their eighties still doing it."

Roy Hunter played basketball for two seasons at North Platte Junior College, met his wife, Denise, and returned to Omaha. In the 1970s he worked at health clubs, gyms, and physical therapy clinics, and became the father of a son, Carlos, and daughter, Robyn. In the early 1980s, Hunter earned bachelors and masters degrees in health and exercise science from the University of Nebraska at Omaha. His resume includes positions at Internorth, Nebraska Department of Health, Pinnacle Health Promotions, Alegent Health, Fremont Area Medical Center, and Blue Cross Blue Shield of Nebraska, for which he appeared in TV ads.

"I feel I've made a difference," Hunter said. "I've touched a lot of lives and had a very rewarding career."

Now a grandfather of four, Hunter on occasion is reminded of the Rhythm Boys.

"I still run into folks who resurrect the nickname," Hunter said. "I think it's neat. It was a unique time and we were a great team. If we had won that last game we would have been considered one of the best teams ever in Nebraska."

John Biddle played basketball for a year at Dana College and won a scholarship to the University of Nevada–Las Vegas, where he played basketball and football and met his wife. After injuries suffered in a car accident cut short his athletic career,

Biddle followed a sister to the University of Minnesota and earned a business degree. He worked for IBM and later for Amdahl Corporation, and was among a group that installed the first ATM machines for Bank of America. A father of two and grandfather of five, Biddle is divorced and lives in Las Vegas. He is a substitute teacher of math and science at the middle-school level.

"I've just enjoyed life—I've been blessed," Biddle said.

Sadie's Home Bakery shut down in 1988. After Biddle's parents passed away, he took ownership of the building on North Twenty-fourth Street. He paid taxes on the property, and maintained it, but it stood empty in 2008, as the Near North Side was mired in commercial stagnation.

"Nobody came up with a commercial plan—I don't think the city wants business on that street," Biddle said, with a note of bitterness. "It all stems from those fires in the sixties. Once that hatred fired up it was there forever. It turned out to be a vendetta against that area."

Willie Frazier was drafted into the U.S. Army after high school, served in Japan as an MP, and played basketball and football for military teams. After he left the service he lost part of an arm in an industrial workplace accident, ran a coffee shop in downtown Omaha, and worked at Veterans Hospital. He lives in Omaha with his wife, Carrie Campbell.

Steve Moss realized his dream of attending Creighton University and played five games for the varsity in 1971. He graduated from Dana College and moved to Anchorage, Alaska, in 1977, where he raised a family and made a career in elementary school education. "I was fortunate to raise my family in Alaska," Moss said. "I come back to Omaha to visit. It's unreal what's happening. I grew up in those neighborhoods—now somebody gets shot every day."

Warren Marquiss taught biology at Central through the 1970s and saw his former basketball understudy, Jim Martin, win back-to-back state championships in 1974 and 1975. He retired in 1981 and succumbed to lung cancer in 2005 at the age of eighty-four. "When he retired he didn't know what the heck to do with himself," said Jim, his son. "He liked being around kids—that was his mission in life."

Vikki Dollis continued her diary into her early twenties. She went to Texas, married, had a son, divorced, remarried, and coped with clinical depression. In the 1990s she went into social work, earned a master's degree from the University of Denver, and became a treatment counselor for public schools in Florence, Colorado. "Reading my high school diaries gave me insight into my students today," Dollis said.

Harvey Josin went into the fabric business with his father and became one of Omaha's Ten Most Eligible Bachelors. He married, raised a daughter and two stepsons, and lives in a Minneapolis suburb.

Jeff Krum went to law school, married and divorced twice, raised a son and daughter, and sells textbooks in the Boston area.

Henry Caruthers married, raised three daughters, worked in warehousing and shipping for the U.S. Post Office, and lives in Omaha.

Jerry Moss lives in San Diego and runs a design and drafting business.

Phil Allison changed his name to Bilal Nosilla and is a social worker in Omaha.

Homer Lee Harris played varsity basketball at Nebraska, married and raised a son, and works as an attorney in New York.

Ralph Hackney died in February 2010.

David L. Rice, who wrote for the *Buffalo Chip*, joined the Black Panther Party, was convicted in the 1970 bombing death of an Omaha police officer, and is serving a life term. He changed his name to Mondo we Langa. His case continues to be controversial because exculpatory evidence was withheld at his trial.

George Wallace served as Alabama's governor from 1971 to 1979 and again from 1983 to 1987. In a 1972 bid for the presidency an assassin's bullet paralyzed him from the waist down, and he made another failed run in 1976. Wallace renounced his racist views in the late 1970s after blacks began to vote in large numbers in Alabama. He died in 1998.

J. Arthur Nelson retired in 1968 and died in 1973. His assistant principal and successor, Gaylord "Doc" Moller, ran Central from 1968 to 1995.

Central's Phil Griffin and Henry Caruthers gaze in astonishment as Dwaine Dillard halts a Benson foe's jump shot.

Coach Warren Marquiss reviews strategy in the decisive victory over "arch rival" Creighton Prep.

Prep's 6'8" Mike Peterson borrows Griffin's shoulder for a boost, but 6'7" Dillard snaps the rebound from over "Pete's" head.

Season's

Central	53	Boys Town	52
Central	62	Tech	63
Central	56	Burke	35
Central	49	South	37
Central	71	Tech	53
Central	70	North	53
Central	63	Westside	51
Central	50	Lincoln	35
Central	64	Thomas Jefferson	54
Central	86	Bellevue	39
Central	64	Abraham Lincoln	61

High - springing Roy Hunter helps Griffin's rebound effort above the heads of Prep's Mathews (25), Haller (23), and Peterson.

The season of the Rhythm Boys as chronicled by the 1968 *Omaha Central High School O-Book*. Reprinted with permission of the *Omaha Central High School O-Book*.

The "Big D" glides down with a snare in victory over Iowa's Abraham Lincoln High.

Record

Central	60	Rummel	49
Central	53	Ryan	46
Central	60	Boys Town	48
Central	61	Prep	48
Central	79	Benson	64
Central	51	Burke	35
Central	73	Bryan	47
Central	66	Benson	43
Central	70	North	51
Central	51	Boys Town	47
Central	50	Lincoln Northeast	54

Willie **Frazier** moves in for the "bound" and Dwaine "does it to 'em." Dillard was the leading rebounder and scorer for the team and placed first on the all-time Central scoring list.

John Biddle flicks for two from about 25 feet in the final with Lincoln Northeast.

Hot-handed Griffin floats a leaping jump shot over the outstretched hands of Lincoln Northeast's Hiatt.

Central adapted and thrived through the end of the last century and into the twenty-first. An Afro-American History course was offered in 1969, and the first Black History Week was held in 1971.

The building, upgraded with new athletic facilities, air conditioning, and conversion of the courtyard into an atrium, was added to the National Register of Historic Places in 1979. The Central High Foundation was founded in 1996 to provide graduates with scholarship support, and the Central High Alumni Association was founded in 1997 to preserve the school's heritage. Susie Buffett's Sherwood Foundation became a generous benefactor.

The basketball team won three straight state championships from 2006 to 2008, another in 2010, and in 2007 Central won a Triple Crown—state titles in football, basketball, and track—a first in Nebraska. Central placed high in the Nebraska Visual Arts Competition, maintained the Road Show tradition, produced an annual musical, and featured strong programs in drama, vocal music, and marching band.

In 2009, Central continued to thrive.

It still attracted students from a broad swath of neighborhoods and remained the most diverse high school in Nebraska, as defined by race, income, religion, national origin, languages spoken at home, and international exchange students.

It finished third for the third consecutive year in the state Academic Decathlon Competition, produced eight National Merit semifinalists, and won the state chess championship for the sixth time in seven years. Central offered twenty-two Advanced Placement courses and a Dual Enrollment Program with the University of Nebraska at Omaha. In the fall of 2009,

Central was on the verge of International Baccalaureate designation, with the goal of offering an IB diploma by 2012–13.

Yet the school was not without its problems. As Principal Greg Emmel told the class of 1969 at its fortieth reunion, "Staff members face huge challenges with apathetic students and parents, gangs, a dropout rate of nearly 30 percent, drugs, violence, mental health and family issues, and poor choices made by the students—the challenges are greater than ever in the history of the school."

Acknowledgments

As a Central High student in 1967–68 I witnessed the season of the Rhythm Boys. Material for this book began with my own recollections.

Many contributed. First was Dwaine Dillard, who in the final weeks of his life gave his encouragement and memories. The support, blessing, and memories of Phyllis Briggs, Carlos Dillard, and Shauntoi Jackson — his mother, brother, and sister — were instrumental.

Likewise Roy Hunter, Phil Griffin, John Biddle, Steve Moss, Bilal Nosilla (the former Phil Allison), Jerry Moss, Harvey Josin, and Jeff Krum, who played on the team, and Dr. Khalid Kamal, who almost played on the team as Lindbergh White.

Jim and Don Marquiss, two sons of the late Warren Marquiss, were generous with their time and memories. Likewise Barbara Essex and Rochelle Dillard, the mothers of three of Dillard's children. Sue Glyn shared her painful memories with courage.

I am indebted to my classmate Vikki Dollis Covington for her diaries, which she excavated from storage, and for her sensitivity and insight, which have always informed her.

Central High's Principal Greg Emmel and archivist Ginny Bauer gave the project an official boost. Jim Wigton of the

Central High Alumni Association provided the annual reports of J. Arthur Nelson, as well as countless other artifacts. The Central High Foundation's Terry Price and Chris Steffen helped me reach out to former students and teachers.

Classmate Marty Johnson, an attorney in Omaha, proved to be a damned good reporter and provided an extra set of eyes, ears, and legs. Photo guru Stuart Cohen worked his magic with the images.

Research included interviews with former administration and faculty members: Dr. Gaylord Moller, Jim Martin, Dan Daly, Mike Gaherty, Clifford Dale, Bob Cain, Bob Whitehouse, and Tim Schmad.

Classmates Delmar Givehand, Darryl Eure, and Bill Graves shared their time and memories.

Also contributing interviews, e-mails, materials, and comments were former students: Akil Secret, Ray Parks, Curt Melton, Larry Cain, Jerry Raznick, Howie Halperin, Bruce Muskin, Tom Milder, Gretchen Menke Anderson, Bob Guss, Jawanda Gauff, Phyllis Mitchell Butler, Vicki Everson West, Harlan Rips, John Gaines, John Grandinetti, Bob Jacobson, Mike Sherman, Gary Soiref, Andy Liberman, Nancy Oostenbrug Roggen, Bonnie Knight Sato, Phil Barth, Nancy Welchert Meyer, Barb Naughtin, Danielle Freeman, Kathy Downs, Mary Campbell, Steve Riekes, Richard Fellman, Geraldine Shafer Romanik, Ron Romanik, Jeri Falk, Susie Buffett, Diana Hahn, Joan Marcus, Jim Kriss, Danny Rubin, and Debbie Gerber Powers.

Other interviewees included Ernie Chambers, Phil Chenier, Ray Schulte, Nate Goodwin, Carrie Campbell, Calvin Webster, Calvin Brown, Lyle Hiatt, Maury Damkroger, Ernie Britt, James

Glass, Conde Sargent, Paul Landow, Hayden West, William Pfeiff, Frank Peak, and Brother Mike Wilmot.

Newspaper archival sources included the *Omaha World-Herald*, *Lincoln Journal Star*, *Omaha Star*, *New York Times*, *North Platte Bulletin*, *Omaha Jewish Press*, *Central High Register*, *Daily Nebraskan*, *Creightonian*, *Buffalo Chip*, and Sun Newspapers of Omaha.

Books about Omaha included *Black and Catholic in Omaha: A Case of Double Jeopardy, the First Fifty Years of St. Benedict the Moor Parish*, by Jack D. Angus (Lincoln NE: iUniverse, 2004); *The Gate City: A History of Omaha*, by Lawrence H. Larsen and Barbara J. Cottrell (Lincoln: University of Nebraska Press, 1997); *The Face of a Naked Lady: An Omaha Family Mystery*, by Michael Rips (New York: Houghton Mifflin, 2005); *Tied to the Great Packing Machine: The Midwest and Meatpacking*, by Wilson Warren (Iowa City: University of Iowa Press, 2007); *I am Third*, by Gale Sayers (New York: Penguin Books, 2001); *Black Quarterback: Marlin Briscoe's Journey to Break the Color Barrier and Start in the NFL*, by Marlin Briscoe (Grand Island NE: Cross Training Publishing, 2002); *Stranger to the Game: The Autobiography of Bob Gibson*, by Bob Gibson (New York: Penguin Books, 1994); *The Color of Class: Poor Whites and the Paradox of Privilege*, by Kirby Moss (Philadelphia: University of Pennsylvania Press, 2003); *The Education of a WASP*, by Lois Mark Stalvey (Madison: University of Wisconsin Press, 1970); *A Thousand Honey Creeks Later: My Life in Music from Basie to Motown*, by Preston Love (Hanover NH: University Press of New England, 1997); *Buffett: The Making of an American Capitalist*, by Roger Lowenstein (New York: Random House, 1995); *The Snowball: Warren Buffett and the Business of Life*, by Alice Schroeder (New York: Random House, 2008); *A. V. Sorensen and The New Omaha*, by Harl A. Dalstrom (Omaha: Lamplighter Press, 1987).

Books about sports included *The Revolt of the Black Athlete*, by Harry Edwards (New York: The Free Press, 1969); *The Black Athlete: A Shameful Story*, by Jack Olsen (New York: Time-Life Books, 1968); and *Satchel: The Life and Times of an American Legend*, by Larry Tye (New York: Random House, 2009).

Books about politics and pop culture included *At Canaan's Edge: America in the King Years 1965–68*, by Taylor Branch (New York: Simon & Schuster, 2006); *Boom! Talking About the Sixties*, by Tom Brokaw (New York: Random House, 2007); *Pictures at a Revolution: Five Movies and the Birth of the New Hollywood*, by Mark Harris (New York: Penguin Press, 2008); and *With Amusement For All: A History of American Popular Culture Since 1930*, by Leroy Ashby (Lexington: University Press of Kentucky, 2006).

The *Central High O-Books* from 1967 to 1969 yielded photos and the footprints of student life. The Nebraska School Activities Association opened its basketball files.

Academic papers included "A Rhetorical Analysis of the Address of Governor George C. Wallace Delivered During the Third-Party State Convention Held in Omaha on March 4, 1968," by Jean Elkon (master's thesis, University of Nebraska at Omaha, 1973); and "Then the Burning Began: Omaha, Riots, and the Growth of Black Radicalism 1966–1969," by Ashley M. Howard (master's thesis, University of Nebraska at Omaha, 2006).

Film sources included the documentaries *A Time For Burning* (1966); *A Street of Dreams* (1994); *'68: The Year Nebraska Mattered* (2008); and *George Wallace: Settin' the Woods on Fire* (2000).

Court records include *State of Nebraska, Appallee, v. Nathaniel Goodwin Jr., Appellant*, no. 37138, Supreme Court of Nebraska, 1969.

Special thanks to Rob Taylor, my editor at University of Nebraska Press, who believed in the story, and disciplined the copy.

On a personal level, my two children, Nora and Alex, suspended disbelief that I was a high school student and followed the project with curiosity.

My wife, Alison Arnett, a career newspaper journalist, gave me a sounding board, executed the first edit, and heard more about Central High than she ever imagined. She is my tutor in adult education. Believe it or not, there's life after high school.

Index